AF540557

CRICKET

DPH SPORTS SERIES

CRICKET

Ashok Kumar

DISCOVERY PUBLISHING HOUSE
New Delhi-110002

First Published-1999
Reprinted-2006

ISBN 81-7141-474-5

© Author

Published by:
DISCOVERY PUBLISHING HOUSE
4831/24, Ansari Road, Prahlad Street,
Daryaganj, New Delhi-110 002 (*INDIA*)
Phone: 3279245
Fax: 91-11-3253475

Printed at:
Arora Offset Press
Laxmi Nagar, Delhi 110 092.

PREFACE

The need of having a sports series felt because today's situation of the world is not conducive to peace, all round there is destruction, despair, conflict and war; war if not between two nations then within the country itself. In a world where there are some 820 million people unemployed or under-employed, and where 86 million people are born every year, it is not surprising that one out of every four individuals lives in absolute poverty. The *Discovery Publishing House* by Publishing this series seeks to get positive response as—to means by which sports can promote and propagate peace and international cooperation. Sportsmen form a large identifiable cadre. We visualises a situation where a conscious efforts is made all over the world to train the sportspersons to spread the message of peace and international cooperation. Instead of peace keeping efforts through arms and army, the sportspersons may be used as soldiers of peace in a subtle manner. The effort is to make the realize the contribution of sports as a factor for sustainable development, peace keeping and international cooperation.

In developing countries, sports development cooperation is still in the need of justification and steadfast arguments. Many people ask the question "why invest in sports in developing countries for which water supply, health service and agriculture projects are much better suited? An apt reply to this question may be "for many of the people of a developing country,

Sports is the only 'Sweaty' Leisure-time activity. Sports represents a moment of joy in the midst of hard poverty-stricken and dirty everyday life. Doing sports even makes one's work go more smoothly the next day.

This series will be useful to the sports promoters, organisers, coaches and other persons related or interested in sports.

Editor

CONTENTS

1

PRACTICE

Probably because it has never been properly defined, cricket practice, in terms of improving performance, has developed in a most illogical way over the years. Many cricketers seem to consider practice not as a means of improving their technique, but more as a light physical work-out. Indeed, we rather suspect that the average practice session does more harm than good to the majority of players. In many instances, it has developed into a social habit; a forerunner to the evening's entertainment! Not that we are saying that this cannot be an enjoyable and worthwhile part of cricketing life; it is, but let us recognise it as that. In fact, following discussions with many keen cricketers it was very conscious of widening interest in cricket practice with a definite objective. Firstly, we must identify what we will be trying to achieve through making a few comparisons. In the normal net practice, any number of different types of bowler may bowl to a batsman for a given period of time, at the end of which there is a general change round and another batsman follows the same routine. In the well-organised practice, with a coach in charge, it is, of course, not so haphazard as we have suggested and there is no doubt that the coach can impart good advice to the players. However, it is one thing listening to advice, but another putting it into practice, especially if the chances of putting the advice into practice are, to say the least, spasmodic. For example, a coach may notice a fault in a batsman when he is trying to drive an off-spinning half volley pitching on middle stump. The coach highlights the fault, shows the batsman how to play the stroke in question, but unfortunately the off-spinner happens to be one of five net bowlers and in the rest of the batsman's quarter of an hour in the net, of the half dozen or less deliveries bowled by the off-spinner, only one is a half volley pitching on middle stump or thereabouts!

In a recent match, the game was lost when the wicket-keeper twice missed stumping the batting team's star batsman in the last over. The bowler in question was a left-arm spin bowler with an unusual spinning action. It was only his second game in the first team. Unfortunately, in the net practice, it was found that there was no room for a wicket-keeper to stand behind the wicket in the net to practise taking the spin bowler. In addition, if it had been possible, the pitch was not very good and bowling with the left-arm spinner was the club's fast opening bowler to whom the wicket-keeper would always stand back anyway.

Again in a recent match, a young fast bowler of whom so much was expected really had a bad time. Not so much in that the batsmen found him easy to score off, but simply because he could not get through his run-up properly. He bowled ten no balls at least. This was not really surprising because he had been doing just that in the previous week's net practice. That is when he could actually get his full run-up in without another bowler getting in his way. On top of this, the young man had bowled for far too long.

Bad coaching - in a quarter of an hour's net practice, a young batsman was corrected on six different strokes in four different positions on each stroke! Might it not have been better for the coach to have concentrated on one fault in maybe two strokes?

In our experience at all levels of the game, realistic, properly defined practice offers the best chance for keen cricketers to improve quickly. Haphazard nets, offering little effective practice, are a sure way of undermining inherent skill and certainly will not assist in the developing of new skills. The examples previously noted are just a few of the situations that prevail in the normal net practice. What is the answer? The whole subject of practice should be reviewed in depth by coaches and cricketers. The message that comes through from everyone is that a much greater emphasis must be put on specific training and practice.

Specific practice

Specific practice means training with a single objective in mind. In so far as cricket is concerned, this means trying to maximise the amount of practice of one skill that can be obtained in a given time. The preceding examples highlight the need to be objective if training is to be worthwhile. In batting, to practise a particular stroke, it is necessary for the ball to pitch within a few inches of a particular spot. If it doesn't, the stroke intended cannot be practised it is as simple as that. It is quite logical, therefore, to ensure that in batting, a weak stroke is practised by dropping, throwing or bowling the ball accurately on to a point on the pitch that will allow the stroke to be played. For convenience, we can create the situation either by using a soft ball on a firm surface possibly indoors, or alternatively by using a cricket ball within the protection of a suitably designed cricket net. Both situations will give considerably more opportunity for the single skill to be practised than would be the case in a normal net practice, where a batsman may not receive one ball to which he could play the stroke he had hoped to practise. In this type of specific practice, whilst it is necessary for the ball to be delivered very accurately, care must be taken not to get too close to the batsman when serving the ball, hence the reason for the net to be suitably designed. A good bowling machine is ideal for specific batting practice. Batsmen should not play the stroke concerned unless they feel the ball has pitched correctly.

Specific practice of bowling is that much easier to control than batting, for obvious reasons. However, it still needs the consideration of sound planning, which means allowing the bowler concerned the freedom of being able to run up and deliver the ball without impedance from others in the bowling area. The same principles apply to fielding and wicket-keeping.

Whether the coach or the cricketer himself makes a conscious effort to improve technique through specific practice, there are still certain requirements without which specific practice will fail to realise its full potential. It may appear to be unnecessarily "fussy", but the very first requirement is to establish a form of recording of progress. The memory is not good enough and I am afraid that whilst it may go against the grain for a practical cricketer, the notebook and pencil are as good as anything, with the exception of the videotape recording, which is by far the best form of recording. If you are not conversant with the possibilities of video, take the time to investigate it will be time well spent.

The first thing to be recorded is an assessment of individual ability as it stands, whether it be for a single skill or the whole range. This means recording strengths in addition to weaknesses. This is not a five minute job, and time should be taken to make a comprehensive assessment. Weaknesses should then be fully analysed and a policy should be established for, or by the individual player. Having established a policy, a programme of training and practice can be compiled and put into operation. At the end of the programme it will be possible to assess its value and look towards further improvements. A word of warning. Do not try too much in the first programme. Look to achieving a small, but definite improvement. A good coach will be a tremendous help to you in achieving your aims, but if a coach is not available, the whole operation can still go ahead with a colleague of similar enthusiasm. The following are examples of specific training and practice in batting and bowling:

Specific training and practice for batting

These can take a very simple form for the individual working with a colleague, or a more sophisticated record form can be designed if working in a group scheme. Personal details should be recorded (age, height, weight etc.), as should the detailed cricket background (record in regular teams etc.). An important section of the notes will be the details of the assessment and the period over which it is considered.

Example assessment

1. Slow footwork.
2. General tendency to play forward too much.
3. No driving power on the off-side considering height and build.
4. Shows no inclination to play horizontal bat strokes off the back foot, probably due to the early forward movement.
5. Grip—top hand too far behind bat handle.
6. Stance—head too far over the off-side and stance too open.
7. Backlift—cramped left (front) arm bending too much, too early.
8. Initial forward movement incorrect and too early. Someone has obviously told him to put his foot to the ball without mentioning head and shoulder as being more important.
9. Initial back movement. On the odd occasion he played back, he opened the body to face the bowler.

Suggested programme

Fitness

Six 30 minute individual circuit training sessions per week for six weeks.

Skills

a) Five half-hour specific practice sessions per week for first two weeks. Off-driving practice only with tennis ball or similar. Two participants only batsman and thrower (plus machine if available).

Check basics periodically. In these sessions practise both check and full follow-through drives.

b) For second two weeks repeat a), but using cricket balls.

c) Final two weeks—five half-hour net practises per week with two selected bowlers, both of whom will be trying to bowl half volleys on or outside the off-stump. The batsman should only play one attacking stroke—the off-drive. Otherwise defend, either forward or back. In the last session record possible dismissals.

The last five net sessions must take place on good pitches, either indoors or outdoors. The emphasis must be on driving the ball with full power. In the group type sessions (first four weeks) when the ball is positioned by throwing or bowling machine, intersperse the normal two-handed backlift by a top handed only backlift.

It is important that a final assessment is undertaken at the end of the programme. In all programmes of training, whether they be self-motivated or group organised, always think in terms of specific practice. If, for example, a bowling machine is available, use it to its best advantage, providing it does the job that you expect from it. At the same time, it should be realised that specific practice does not mean selfish practice. When assisting a colleague, it simply means that the assistant is taking his turn to provide the maximum realistic practice conditions possible.

Practice for bowling

Assessment notes

General assessment details are as for batting,

depending upon whether monitoring is by group or individual, for example:

Example assessment

Both net sessions were video recorded. Matches were recorded by tape recorder and notebook. It was noticeable in both cases that as the bowler tired, direction suffered, rather than length. Over thirty per cent of deliveries pitched on and outside the leg-stump in the second half of both matches and practice sessions. Run-up is inconsistent, on occasions losing rhythm, possibly through a shortened stride approaching delivery. The bowler's quite lively pace comes from a fast arm action at delivery. His action at the wicket is quite good, but strained through his poor run-up. He does not seem to have any bowling plan and it is difficult to see what type of delivery he is trying to bowl.

Programme

Three half-hour physical training sessions per week for all six weeks. A new training programme should be embarked upon at the beginning of next year, leading him into the season fully fit for real progress as a fast bowler. In conjunction with, or separate to the weekly physical training sessions, effort should be made to go through the following minimum programme of technique improvement:

First three weeks

Five half-hour net sessions per week (no batsman). First fifteen minutes should be concentrated on developing new run-up. The new run-up should be established in consultation with a good coach, if possible. If not, follow good written advice on the subject. Short strides to long strides with acceleration and rhythm should be the theme. Study leading international bowlers. The remaining fifteen minutes should be concentrated on hitting a set target (1' wide x 2') positioned on a suitable length just outside the off-stump (using the new style run-up). Continually check basic action and look to develop swing bowling technique.

Second three weeks

Five one hour net sessions with batsman. Practice should not be with more than one other bowler and even then, the two bowlers should bowl six balls each consecutively (one over) as in a match. This will allow the over to be planned. Video record, if possible, but in any case, thoroughly analyse the whole practice.

The methods described can be adapted and improved upon with experience. Fielding and wicket-keeping practice can be accommodated into specific practice. Take care not to let specific training and practice dominate to the exclusion of other forms of practice and the playing of cricket games for fun and practice. In fact, specific practice can be integrated into some of the excellent cricket games that are now part of the cricket scene.

The National Cricket Association's Proficiency Award Scheme Tests are also excellent training in the skills of cricket for eight to eighteen year olds and provide much fun in addition to giving a sound measure of improvement in technique. Always try to make practice interesting. Divide your practice time to allow variation in activity and always commence with a warm-up session.

Measured cricket practice

Based on the principles of Group Coaching and Circuit Training, we found this method of practising to be very effective, as it simulates the combinations of requirements needed for improving skills. For example, it:

1. Gives skill practice in a variety of environments in or out of doors, obviating the need for a special cricket facility.
2. Measures skill improvement by setting achievable targets.
3. Improves physical fitness.
4. Improves concentration,

All the skills of cricket can be simulated by setting up the required situation for the performing of the particular skill. It is important to define exactly what skill is to be practised and care should be taken that markers and floor markings are repositioned exactly when the practice of the skill is repeated. A record of performance should be made during each practice session, i.e. number of balls hit between the markers, number of deliveries hitting the target area when bowling, etc. A challenge is then set and improvement, if any, can be gauged. Take particular note of any variations in pattern of performance over a long practice session, i.e. in the first two overs of a ten over bowling spot. It is a good idea for young players to keep a book recording their performances in all forms of training. Comparison may be made between this type of practice and the cricket circuit suggested in the Fitness chapter. Remember that there is a vital difference. In this instance, correct technique and success in directing the ball is the criterion. In the cricket circuit, speed of correct performance is the criterion, time being the measured ingredient. When laying out the practice area and setting markers, take care to make the size and distance apart of the markers commensurate with ability. Always set an achievable goal, if not an easy one.

Cricket games for practice

Pairs and Eight-a-Side Cricket are marvellous cricket innovations giving enjoyable practice, as well as competition to players of all ages. They are games that are used too infrequently in the development of the game and its skills. Their greatest function is that they provide action for everyone. They are games that can be played in or out of doors, in sports halls or on cricket grounds, and they can be enjoyed using a soft or a hard ball.

Pairs cricket

The game is played in competition between pairs. In practice it can be designed to give practice to pairs of players in any of the game's skills. In a practice session for example, twelve players could follow the playing sequence to cover the time available. Any combination of pairs could be arranged. For example, if a form of specific practice was required, six batsmen could form three pairs and six bowlers could form three pairs, each pair rotating after an agreed number of overs.

In general, the rules of cricket would apply. Each pair bat for an agreed number of overs, regardless of whether they are dismissed or not. If a batsman is dismissed, an agreed number of runs is deducted from his score, which commences with a total of one hundred. The deductable total can be set for any occasion, although eight has been found suitable for players under fourteen years of age and ten, twelve or more for older players. In a practice session, scores need not be kept, although it is recommended that they should be to add the element of match play so necessary in practice.

Eight-a-side cricket

As good as anything for both team practice and competition, Eight-a-Side Cricket is an extension of pairs cricket. Eight players (four pairs) form a team, each pair batting for an agreed number of overs. The team score commences with a total of two hundred. There is no need for individual scores to be, kept; simply deduct an agreed number from the team total when a wicket falls: In its simplest form of practice, scores can be called after every score or wicket, by the umpire.

As can be imagined, there is a much greater accent on fielding in this game, as compared to eleven-a-side cricket, and as such, improvement in ground fielding can be spectacular.

Rules

The Laws of Cricket shall apply with the following exceptions:

1. Each team shall comprise eight players.
2. Each game shall consist of one innings per team, each innings to be of sixteen overs duration (twenty overs when time permits, or twelve overs when time is limited).

3. The batting side shall be divided into pairs, each pair batting for four overs and changing at the end of the fourth, eighth and twelfth over. In a twenty over game, at the end of the fifth, tenth and fifteenth over. In a twelve over game, at the end of the third, sixth and ninth over.

4. Batsmen shall have unlimited "lives", but each life shall result in eight runs (this may be varied, depending on the age group) being deducted from the total. Batsmen shall change ends at the fall of each wicket, except on the last ball of an over.

5. Each player on the fielding side must bowl, with the exception of the wicket-keeper. No player shall bowl more than three overs (four overs in a twenty over game).

6. Each team shall commence its innings with a score of 200 runs.

7. The winning team shall be the side scoring the higher number of runs after deductions for the fall of wickets.

8. In all matches no fielder, except the wicket-keeper, shall be allowed to field nearer than eleven yards, measured from the middle stump, except behind the wicket on the off-side.

Duration of games

Pairs and Eight-a-Side Cricket Games can be played within various limited periods of time. When arranging a match, organisers should emphasise the importance of not wasting time in changing over etc., i.e. a sixteen over match can be completed easily within two hours; twelve overs within one and a half hours, etc. We can see this game taking place at the highest level. Imagine spectators having the opportunity of seeing sixteen Test players displaying their skills all within two or three hours.

Continuous cricket

This is a fun game that can be ideal for finishing off a practice or training session, when time is too short to organise a pairs game. Whilst it is purely a fun game and has little to offer batsmen or bowlers in serious practice, there is ample scope to develop sound fielding techniques, providing there are not too many players,

Rules

1. Number of complete innings per team should be decided before commencement of the game.
2. The ball must be delivered underhand to bounce no more than once before the wicket.
3. The bowler may bowl, whether or not a batsman is at the wicket.
4. The batsman must run every time he hits the ball.
5. To score a run, the batsman must run round the skittle and be in position to play a stroke at the next ball delivered.
6. A batsman can be "out" bowled, or caught only.
7. The umpire must call "out" immediately the batsman is dismissed.
8. The incoming batsman must remain seated on the

batting chair until the previous batsman is given "out".

9. The umpire must call "No Ball" if the ball bounces more than once before reaching the wicket, or if the bowler delivers the ball in front of the bowling mark.

2

FITNESS

There is no doubt that the cricketer of today is much fitter than his counterpart of not many years ago. This is not to say that most cricketers of today are as fit as they might be. In fact physical fitness training for cricketers is a comparatively recent innovation. Together with practice, fitness training is an area that still has much to offer in improving a player's performance, although at the highest levels of cricket, I must say that fielding has become something of a spectator sport in itself. In general however, the lack of success from apparently talented players can very often be traced to a lack of physical fitness. Skills are at their best in their initial performance but can quickly break down under sustained physical pressure. Having said this, let me hasten to add that physical fitness can only play a limited role in the success of a cricketer. A knowledge of and an ability to perform the skills of the game will always lead the way and fitness as such will only ever be an assistance to maintaining the quality and quantity of those skills. In fitness training, especially outside the cricket season, there is much enjoyment in players getting together as a group or team. Training sessions help players get to know each other and can only help to make the game in the summer so much better collectively as well as individually. The importance of fitness can easily be recognised in any number of cricket situations. Just consider yourself, for example. Can you honestly say that, immediately after running the second or third consecutive three runs in an over, you are just as likely to score off or even survive the next ball with the certainty you did the first of the over? If the bowler knows his job he will be giving you much time to recover. What chance do you think a bowler has of bowling at his best if he cannot cope with a chase or two around the boundary edge between overs? How do you think the odds change on a wicket-keeper missing a catch in the first over through lack of concentration after he has batted for two or three hours just previously?

Warming up

When it is known that any exercise is to take place requiring maximum effort, whether it be in training or in a match, warming up exercises should be undertaken. This reduces the possibility of injury. The warm-up should produce a "slight sweating" condition through such physical activities as light jogging or easy general exercises. The light practice of fielding skills can provide a more interesting warm-up.

Specific training

Specific training like specific practice is the most desirable and effective training for a cricketer. Specific circuit training programmes can be designed by the coaches or the individual with a little experience and research. Specialists in Physical education are always willing to help Particular sports in this respect. This type of programme will bring a player up to a satisfactory standard of fitness without over-emphasis on fitness as against skill training,

Circuit training

Circuit training in cricket is a simple method of giving a player a variety of exercises that will improve the three main functions relating to his performance on the field. These are strength, endurance, and mobility. Circuit training suits the cricketer very well in that it is realistic and enables the player to keep within his physical capabilities.

Procedure for establishing a circuit

A programme is designed covering say eight exercises, each relating to cricket skills a player is likely to perform. Each exercise is practised until proficiency is achieved. The number of repetitions achieved on each exercise in say 60 seconds is recorded. This number is then halved and performed in two thirds of the time i.e. 40 seconds. The whole circuit may then be repeated a set number, say three times, trying to maintain the target time of 40 seconds per exercise. Players work at achieving this target time and in doing so build an increasingly better standard of fitness. When the target time is achieved the programme can be intensified by reducing the target time or by increasing the number of repetitions. Alternatively a new circuit can be designed.

Important

If there is any reason to think that the exercises in a programme are too strenuous, qualified advice should be sought. In very fit young cricketers training can take place at up to 180 heart beats per minute. In general it is inadvisable to go beyond 150. Weight training

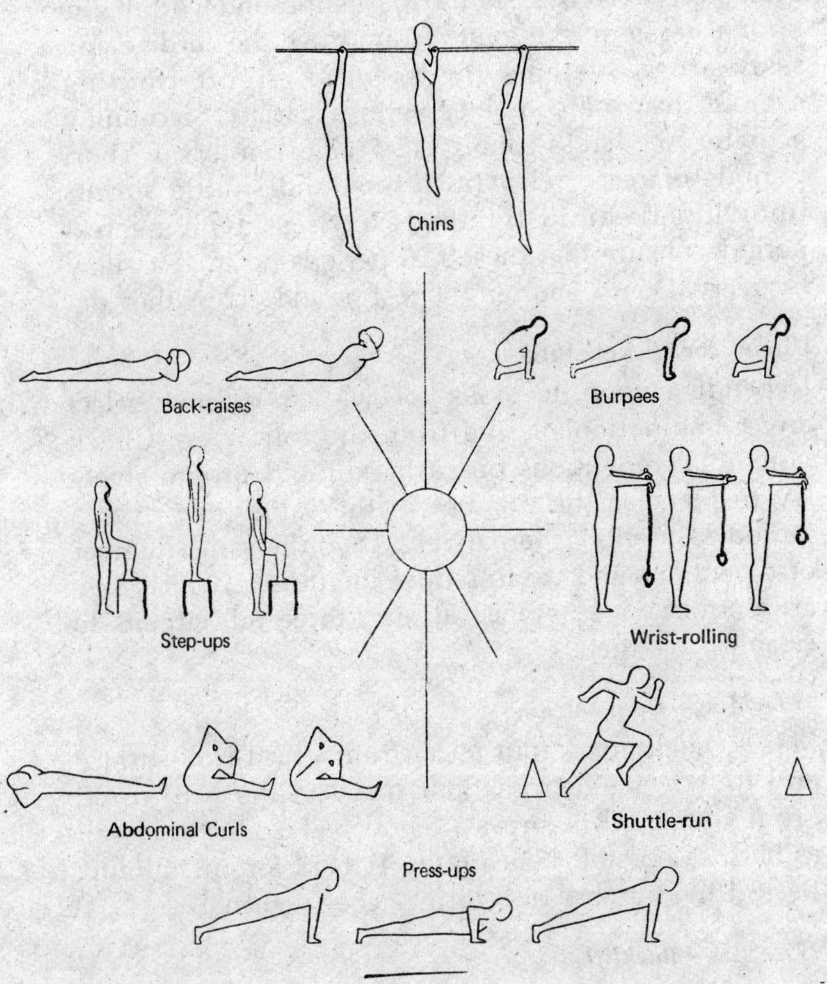

A useful training circuit for cricketers without the use of special equipment

should only be carried out under qualified instruction. Stretching exercises should be gentle and within the normal range of the joint. To improve the cardiac and respiratory systems the specific circuit training exercises can be combined with a variety of running activities, i.e. cross-country (2-5 miles), interval (short periods of rest), relay (in teams) and shuttle sprints (individual). In all training exercises involving rest periods, ensure that these rest periods do in fact allow recovery. Do no, shorten the rest period unless they do.

Circuit for cricket skills

Depending upon the skills you wish to practise, select any combination of five from the following. Check your total repetitions on each skill and progressively try to increase the number in the same time over a period of weeks. Alternatively, keep the same number of repetitions and try to reduce the time in which they are performed. Complete at least three full circuits to establish a target.

1) Fielding—close catching

Make a chalk mark four paces from a firm wall surface and four feet (4') from floor level on the wall itself. From your marker throw a tennis ball against the wall as hard as possible beneath the 4′ mark for one minute. Record the number of return catches you make.

2) Batting—Backlift

Set a string or rope horizontally at head height. Take your normal stance with your front shoulder pointing away from the string so that when completing a full backlift the bottom of your bat just touches the string. Record the number of correct backlifts you make from the correct stance in one minute.

3) Bowling action

Set up two sets of wickets or larger targets 22 yds apart marking the creases at both ends with chalk. Take your normal run, select a ball from a container placed at the beginning of your run. Bowl normally, but after your follow-through run to the other end and repeat. Record the number of good deliveries (pitching on a marker) you make in one minute.

4) Running between wickets

Bat in hand run between markers set 20 yds apart touching down with the bat as you would in a match. Record the number of runs in one minute.

5) Fielding—stop and throw

Position a bucket of tennis balls a minimum of 30 paces from a firm, plain wall. Throw one ball at the wall over a height of 8' if possible, field the return in the long barrier position and throw again from the same distance. Record the number of correct throws made in one minute.

6) Fielding—Retrieving

Again mark at least 8′ from the floor on a firm plain wall and make a large target above the line. Line up a number of tennis balls next to each other on a line 20' from the wall. From back to the wall position run to the first ball, pick up and throw as quickly as possible over the 8' mark, at the target. Return to the wall and repeat as many times as possible in the minute. Record the number of correct throws that hit the target.

7) Batting—Lofted drive

Chalk or fix a large circular "bulls eye" on a wall at least 10' high if possible. Mark a batting crease approximately 20' away and facing the target. Bouncing a tennis ball at will try to hit the target with a lofted straight drive. Repeat, always commencing from a good stance position at the crease. Record the number of strokes made in one minute. (The straighter and harder the hit the quicker the ball will return.)

8) Bowling—Action

From the "coil" position bowl a tennis ball from a line 10 yds away from the wall, as hard as possible to bounce over a line marked 4' from the floor on the wall. Collect the ball as quickly as possible. Record the number of correct deliveries made in one minute.

9) Wicket-keeping or slip catching

Set a string or chalk line on a wall just high enough to touch with the outstretched fingers from a squat jump. From the wicket-keeper's squatting position jump and touch the line as many times as possible in one minute. Record the number of successes.

With a little initiative this type of cricket circuit can easily be adapted for pairs or small groups. For example, with Item 1 close catching can be done in pairs. With Item 3 bowlers can bowl to each other.

In all specific training care must be taken to ensure that the cricket skill is performed correctly. Bad habits can easily be developed and it is recommended that a good coach be on hand whenever possible.

3

COACHING

Watching a Test match between England and Australia an experienced observer would not need to know the players or see the colour of their caps to realise which side was batting. May be the playing conditions in the respective countries have something to do with it but in my view the major factor is coaching. Most Englishmen arc coached from an early age. Not only that but the coach is very often an ex-professional who played for his county over a long period and in turn was coached at the start of his career.

Australians, by comparison, receive very little coaching. When they do, particularly at the club level, the coach is frequently one of the team. He is possibly a batsman who received no coaching himself as a boy.

Inevitably this lack of coaching means that players develop along more natural but less orthodox lines. The coaching which does take place is directed rather more towards what to do with the ball than how to do it. There is not so much insistence on the left elbow forward or the straight back lift in batting.

Regrettably in a large proportion of schools there is often no coach or sports-master who has any special knowledge, and his assistance to the boys can only be of a general character. Recently very strenuous efforts have been made by the major Australian associations to improve this state of affairs. The use of films for instructional purposes, the holding of clinics for schoolboys, the organisation of schoolboy competitions and such like are being encouraged and this is good, but the effects cannot be apparent immediately.

Professional cricket as practised in England has never existed in Australia. There has not been enough cricket to sustain it.

Apart from the occasional player who spent a season with the Lancashire League (and this was usually done to gain experience as much as money) all Australian players earned their livelihood at some other occupation, be it bank clerk, agent, electrician, etc. It was often difficult to convince English people of this situation. Many players in fact suffered in their private occupations by giving much time to the game. Lack of promotion, as compared with colleagues who put in more time at their jobs, was sometimes the result.

The evolution of cricket systems in all countries is bound to see changes which cannot be accurately predicted at this stage.

In a country like Australia, where the wickets are hard and fairly true, there is not such a premium on correct batting technique as there is in England. Many of our young players find on going overseas that they have to make certain adjustments and play more correctly to cope with the ever-changing conditions abroad and all Australians need the experience of an English tour to tighten up their defence.

Some coaches try to alter a player's basic natural gifts, which is quite wrong unless there is some glaring fault certain to bring disaster. There is no sense in making a bowler grip the ball a certain way to bowl a leg-break if he can spin it better and obtain greater accuracy by his own unorthodox grip. It is dangerous to suppress originality and enterprise just for the sake of orthodoxy. Coaches must have the sense to understand when there is need for correction and when it is better to keep quiet.

And they must be sure not to overcoach. Denis Compton who, in commenting on coaching, had this to say.

"If a young player with a good eye and a gift for the game has some unorthodox shot which is nevertheless always successful, it is wrong to coach him out of it. To do so deprives the batsman of the initiative and the onlookers of the pleasure they get from watching some originality."

The text books may say a batsman's back lift should be straight. Within reason that is true--for defensive play anyway. But mine wasn't, and if we had been compelled to take my bat back on a perfectly straight line when intending to play the pull shot, could never have done it.

The basic technique of a straight bat is sound for defence but there should be all possible emphasis on attack, on the aggressive outlook. And if technique is going to prove the master of the player and not his servant, then it will not be doing its job.

Think of some of the great batsmen and you will find very few who did not depart in some major degree from orthodoxy. Sir Leonard Hutton and Sir Jack Hobbs were two renowned masters of style and correctness (though you may be surprised to know Jack Hobbs was not coached). But what of Denis Compton, Bill Ponsford and men of that ilk? They were ever ready to back their judgment and eyesight if the occasion demanded.

As we have often remarked, "You wouldn't attempt to teach a man billiards on a table that wasn't level." I'm afraid some of the people charged with the responsibility of providing practice wickets on suburban grounds think any old piece of turf upon which a roller has been used will suffice.

It is an unfortunate outlook. Many a young player has had his confidence shattered by a nasty blow in the face. A bumpy pitch and a fast bowler and you have the first ingredients of "backing away," the greatest mistake any batsman can make.

And, as W. G. Grace maintained over half a century ago, it is much harder to produce attractive stroke players when the pitches are bad.

The faster and truer they are, the easier your batsmen will learn the fundamentals of stroke play.

Unsatisfactory turf pitches are the main reason why we see a good deal of merit in hard wickets. We learnt my cricket on concrete, with coir or canvas mat covering, and know its limitations. There is no substitute for good turf. But to teach young lads the rudiments of stroke play it is most helpful that there should be some uniformity in the behaviour of the ball. Some of the experimental pitches which are a combination of rubber and bitumen (or similar mixture) offer considerable promise. They have the advantage that no watering and rolling is required and the cost of maintenance is negligible. From time to time evidence is forthcoming that Australian batsmen do not show to advantage when confronted by a wet wicket. This is usually followed by suggestions that wet wickets should be provided for practice in Australia. The people who propound the idea have seldom had any experience of batting under those conditions.

In England a wet wicket does not necessarily mean a bad one. In fact, very often a dry wicket over there is materially improved by rain. The English turf seldom takes on any viciousness. The ball will turn, but turn slowly. It will lift, but not alarmingly, and there is definitely some possibility that a sound technique and a certain amount of ability will enable one to overcome the conditions.

The chances of doing so in Australia are much more i mote. There one finds the ball will turn quickly and fly up very abruptly. It becomes as much a question of self-protection as batting technique.

Few players are willing to take the physical hiding which survival entails unless the occasion demands it, and frequently a reasonable score is more likely to be compiled by a few minutes lusty swinging than by scientific play.

Would you like to run the risk (not a remote chance but a distinct probability) of being hit on the jaw by a cricket ball doing 6070 miles an hour? And if you say, "Well, let only the slow bowlers have a go," the answer is that when it comes to matches you are almost sure, under today's playing conditions, to find yourself up against a quickish bowler. The groundsman, too, dislikes players bowling on wet wickets because in Australia the ball cuts up the turf so much, and that same practice strip very often has to be used for weeks on end.

In theory the idea sounds fine and in England it probably happens often in the natural course of events, but in Australia I'm afraid the batsmen are unlikely to face it for pleasure.

At Adelaide there is now a delightful arrangement whereby the players may conveniently go down the steps at the rear of the stand and within fifty yards they are able to enter a cyclone enclosure which is self-contained and entirely set aside for practice and coaching. This is used before big games, and is also used on mornings before play begins and during the day whilst play is in progress. It is especially helpful in that batsmen, say Nos. 5 and 6 can go and have a lengthy practice whilst Nos. 1, 2 or 3 are at the wickets. In that way they play under exactly the same light and probably on a pitch resembling in character the one in the middle.

For touring teams it provides a convenient opportunity for practice during the day for those players who are not participating in the current match. These things are denied to players where the only practice facilities are on the playing arena.

Practice areas should always have a safety arbour where players can pad up without the constant need to watch out for the ball, and authorities should be careful to see the nets are foolproof. Just one hole might bring a casualty such as the broken jaw Bill Alley suffered one day when a full-blooded hook from the chap next door went straight through and felled him. It is a good idea to use the practice nets for really solid practice. Far too many players use them for exercise only.

It always annoys me to see a batsman hitting balls away out of the net, making no attempt to improve his game and being a thorough nuisance to the bowlers and the other players who have to retrieve the ball. That is not the place for slogging.

Batsmen should see to it that they get opportunities for batting against the type of bowling they dislike or find difficulty in playing. Bowlers should measure out their proper run and treat the matter seriously. This is to their own advantage and anything else is unfair to the batsman who can hardly improve his technique against bowlers who are fooling.

There is a tendency these days to neglect fielding practice. We don't think an outfield needs to have much work, especially in catching, because too many catches at the one time can make the hands sore and cause you to flinch. But there should always be a few. The infields need plenty. Slip-catching machines are a useful adjunct even though they have their limitations. One soon gets accustomed to the machine and can tell which way the ball will come off it. That is exactly what you can't do in a match.

But irrespective of whatever else he may do and whatever specialised training he may indulge in, I think there is nothing better than constant playing with a ball.

We don't care whether it is a tennis ball, a golf ball, baseball or any other medium. Nor do I mind the size and shape of the bat. It may be not even a bat at all, but only a golf ball and a piece of wood. The thing is that playing with a ball of any kind teaches ball sense. You acquire a sort of automatic knowledge of what reaction there is when a ball with a certain spin on it hits a solid object.

The more one can do things instinctively and have less cause to worry about what a ball might do--the more you can be certain of your judgment of its flight in the air instead of distrusting yourself--the greater will be your confidence. If a player is consistently compiling big scores and has sore hands, he may have good reason for reducing his net practice.

Watch others, note their methods and learn by observation and example.

Coaches themselves must be very careful not to stultify the natural gifts of youngsters and must realise they can't turn every player into a robot. Whilst watching net practice we have recently seen some bad examples. A youngster played a delightful pull shot and was promptly carpeted by the coach because he dared to hit a ball from outside the off stump to the on side. What do you think that did to his initiative?

Another boy was forced to stand with his feet together when his natural stance (with feet apart) was ideal--that is, ideal for playing cricket but not for his coach.

And then there's the chap who insists that every drive shall be made after the ball passes the front leg. Some coach could show how to play an on drive that way. It is a mistake to fog a boy's mind with a multiplicity of complicated instructions, which means he forgets the much more important and simple basic principles.

And so could go on about the question of using judgment. The coach must be careful because he is usually the old master teaching a pupil, but the proteges should also think and be sure they don't slavishly accept everything as being correct just because someone tells them so. They in turn must play their part. In the final analysis, the best teacher is yourself Analyse things sensibly--work out what suits you personally--practise and observe. No coach on earth can give you ability or judgment. He can only tell you what to do or how to do it. The execution rests entirely with you.

When Martin Donnelly (the great New Zealand left-hand batsman) first went to England, the team worked out on the boat going over how they would play, in theory. After getting away to a bad start and putting up some poor performances their captain said to them, "I've listened to all you fellows talking theory since we left home. Go out to the nets this afternoon and forget all that and for goodness sake just look hard at the ball and hit it."

We cannot emphasize too much my belief that "watching the ball" and "concentration" are of greater importance than all the theories.

Finally, we should add that in Australia the difficulty of finding a suitable coach for a state association is very real and so is the problem of adequate financial recompense.

It is a tribute to the long sightedness of this Government that it appreciates what cricket can mean to a British speaking community.

Perhaps the presence of Cyril Merry and Learie Constantine in the Government offers the explanation.

Public funds are spent in many less worthy ways.

Running between the wickets

One of the most exhilarating experiences for a cricket spectator is to watch a partnership between two batsmen who never miss an opportunity of picking up the cheekiest of singles. Good running is largely a matter of judgment and experience. When two great players such as Hobbs and Sutcliffe have enjoyed countless hours together at the wicket they build up a marvellous understanding and a confidence in each other which makes the task appear simple.

But the hallmark of a really good runner is that he shall be able to run well with anybody. That can only be achieved by a strict observance of sound principles.

The ground is very often rough so that the bat cannot be slid along the turf at the conclusion of a run- -the running surface alongside the pitch is uneven and the average country player just hasn't had the experience.

It was arranged that we should bat together whenever possible. We ran him out and he ran me out but the matches were unimportant so that didn't matter. The lessons were absorbed and stood by me in later life. It is generally accepted that the striker is responsible for calling when the ball is hit in front of the wicket, whilst the non-striker shall call for a stroke behind the wicket. However, that must be regarded as a generalisation only. Either party must obviously have the right to deny his partner's call if he sees it is too dangerous.

Take a drive into the covers. The striker plays forward, moves into his shot and begins to advance down the pitch as fie calls. But his partner slips a trifle in starting to run and notices that cover has made rapid progress towards the ball, which is seen going to his right hand, and the signs point towards a swift return to the wicket-keeper. The non-striker thinks he has no hope of making his ground.

He would obviously be foolish to go on with the run just because theoretically it was the right thing to do, according to the textbook. He would have a duty to call "No" immediately so that not only would he be protecting himself but he would also give his partner ample time to stop and return to the crease.

In such a case it is important that the denial of the striker's call must be loud, clear and prompt.

Under all circumstances initial calling, whether by striker or non-striker, should be restricted to one of three words, "yes," "no" or "wait," and every call must be decisive.

You might say, "How can the call of wait be decisive?" Well it can be in this sense, that the other person is effectively stopped from continuing a run pending some development.

Supposing a hard cover drive is made wide of the fieldsman, who can only hope to field it one handed. Both batsmen make preliminary moves towards running, but the striker realises that a hard drive to cover is more likely to produce a run-out than one hit slowly. He therefore prefers to wait and see whether the ball is cleanly picked up or whether the fieldsman overruns it before being willing to commit himself.

Cases like this usually produce a dangerous run or an easy one, depending entirely on whether the ball is fielded cleanly. So the value of the "wait" call in this instance is to protect the non-striker from any danger of a run-out and at the same time warn him to be at the ready should the opportunity occur to continue the run.

There are lots of ways in which the two batsmen at the wickets can help each other. Assume a ball is cut down the gully and the batsmen set off for a run. By the time they cross on the first run, the non-striker should be able to form a fairly clear judgment as to whether the stroke will yield more than a single. So on passing the striker (whose back is towards the ball) he may say, "Probably two," or some such guiding remark. This immediately gives his partner the cue to turn quickly at the end of the first run and be ready to decide immediately whether he is willing to come back towards the dangerous end for a second. The call for that second run would be the prerogative of the striker who would be returning to the wicket most likely to be endangered.

The one unforgiveable sin in running is indecision. There is nothing worse than a shilly-shally in mid-pitch with neither man knowing what the other proposes to do--the sort of thing a friend of mine describes as a "perfect misunderstanding". If in doubt say "No". Only in exceptional circumstances is one run worth the risk of a valuable wicket.

After much experience with another player, expert runners can largely dispense with calling because of mutual understanding.

Pay due regard to the speed of your partner. It is essential to make sure as far as possible that each run is just as safe for him as it is for you. That wonderful judgment of pace and distance which some men possess can be developed up to a point, though not everyone can hope to attain it. But everybody can acquire certain basic knowledge of procedure which should invariably be followed.

1. The non-striker should always backup. He does not have to stand behind the crease. So long as the bat is grounded behind, that is sufficient. We made a practice of standing outside with the bat inside as demonstrated by the photograph, and we moved off immediately and saw the ball in the air after it had left the bowler's hand.

Some players have adopted the habit of moving off as the bowler completes his run. The danger of this method is that the bowler is quite entitled to retain the ball (as his arm goes over in the delivery stride) and knock the bails off at the bowling end. If the non-striker is then out of his ground he is run-out.

Some people frown on this practice as being sharp, and think the bowler should first issue a warning. I cannot see this at all. The non-striker, by backing up too far or too soon, is in effect cheating. He is gaining an unfair advantage which may save him being run-out in a photo finish the other end.

The law clearly provides that the non-striker may be run out at the bowler's end if he prematurely leaves his ground, and I have seen it happen in Test cricket. Hence my dictum--watch for the ball in the air before leaving the safety zone.

2. The non-striker should always stand two or three yards wide of the return crease on the opposite side of the stumps to that from which the bowler is delivering the ball.
3. The striker should always run closer to the pitch than the non-striker. Let me make this one clearer. To a right-hand batsman, with a left-hander bowling over the wicket, the non-striker would stand on the off-side of the pitch. Should the striker play a cover drive which, by virtue of his movement, takes him over to the off-side, he too will run down that side. He should then run as close as possible to the pitch (without running on it, of course) and the non-striker should be on the outside of him. With such an understanding there is no danger of a collision or doubt about which lane to run in.

It would be wrong in such circumstances for the striker to cut across the pitch after making his shot, just in order to run down the leg side. But if he jumped down the wicket to play an on drive, he may find it easier and more convenient to continue down the on side. There can be no absolute hard-and-fast rule about which side of the pitch the striker should run. That is so often decided by circumstances. It is the non-striker's job to give his partner ample room and to protect him.

4. In making good his crease each batsman should ground his bat short of the popping crease and

slide it over. This is particularly important, when attempting to avoid a run-out or when making a quick turn for a second run. There is no need for the feet to reach the crease. They may well stop a good yard short and that is ground saved. In fact, having regard to the starting position of the non-striker when he may stand outside his crease, and the distance he saves the other end, he only has to run some 18 yards.

5. As a general principle, run the first one fast in case there may be a chance of another. This must be interpreted with common sense. Plenty of shots are made where it is clearly impossible for more than one run to be scored. It would be absurd in such cases for the batsmen to wildly charge up the pitch looking for another run and merely help deplete their physical resources. On the other hand a glance to fine-leg where there is a fieldsman on the fence may well provide two runs if there is a semblance of misfielding, and the striker would need to get to the bowler's end quickly, turn and be ready for the chance,

6. Having completed a run and in the process of turning for a second, always turn towards that side of the ground on which the ball is struck. This may sound complicated but it isn't. The photographs clearly show what I mean.

A right-handed striker who makes a cover drive should, on turning for the second run, ground the bat with his left hand and turn towards cover. When making an on drive he would ground the bat with his right hand and turn towards the on side.

You may think such a point is trivial. It is not. Most run-outs occur by the narrowest of margins and these refinements are the very things which make all the difference. Good running is a joy to watch and an even greater joy to implement. Its dangers lie in slow starting and indecision. If both batsmen run immediately the ball is struck, it is amazing what they can achieve and how difficult it becomes to run them out.

And don't overlook the great value of running between wickets as an adjunct to disorganisation of an attack and a fielding plan.

So long as the covers may remain deep and short runs are not taken, so long will they enjoy the advantage of being able to cut off fours which otherwise might get through. Judicious short running may pull them in and provide major scoring opportunities.

With a left and a right-hand batsman operating together, the constant scoring of singles causes the field to change over and forces the bowler to repeatedly change his direction. No bowler Ekes that and very few can prevent it having some effect on their accuracy.

Batsmen should observe which fields-men are quick, which are slow, who can throw fast, who can't, whether a man is right or left-handed, whether he is approaching the ball on his throwing side or not. There is literally no end to the subject.

Quite recently we were amused when two chaps were going for a run and the striker called out so loudly we heard him in the pavilion, "Come two--he has a glass arm." The same result could have been achieved without embarrassing the fieldsman and revealing to the fielding captain what he had observed. Even though a run-out appears inevitable, never give up. Many a batsman has made his ground safely because the wicket-keeper, in his excitement over a chance, has fumbled the ball, or when the fieldsman has failed to gather cleanly or thrown wildly in his urgent attempt to beat the batsman. If you give up the chase, you give added time and confidence to the fielding side who are less likely then to fall into error.

Should you accidentally drop the bat in running, it is mostly quicker to keep going than to stop and retrieve it. The bat can be safely picked up after the run is completed.

Despite every precaution run-outs will occur. More often than not no doubt exists as to who is to be the victim. But occasionally, through a misunderstanding, both batsmen find themselves in the middle and a run-out for somebody is inevitable.

If one of them is a recognised first-class bat and the other a rabbit, the latter should immediately sacrifice his own wicket by making certain he gets into the position which ensures he gets trapped. That is one of the rare cases where, in the interests of the team, the better batsman has a right to be selfish and allow his partner to be sacrificed.

Finally, don't forget to learn the rule about a substitute runner. You never know when (a) you may need one or (b) when your partner may need one and you will have to run with him. It would be a pity if you were run-out simply because you didn't realise that when striking, both you and your substitute are vulnerable. The striker may be out stumped or run-out even though his substitute runner is behind the crease. And the striker may be out if his substitute is guilty of "handling the ball" or "obstructing the field".

It takes a long time to become a really first-class runner, but do urge all players to realise the importance of this phase of cricket. There is great pleasure to be derived from it, apart altogether from the rewards.

4

EQUIPMENT

Something we have noticed about the most successful players and teams is the way they are turned out. Looking the part is halfway towards playing the part and time and time again this adage is proved in matches. Nothing gives a team more of a "boost" than to find they are playing against a team who obviously do not care about their appearance. Successful players have pride and whether it be in performance or appearance, it should naturally become an integral part of any young player's development. Looking the part does not mean that every item of equipment must be the most expensive there is, it only means that it should be clean and well serviced. Young cricketers are very often persuaded to invest their hard earned savings in cheap equipment that looks well on the outside, but is shoddy on the inside. Take great care when selecting equipment. List the priorities and make sure that once equipment has been purchased, you also have the backup materials to service it properly.

Bats and footwear are particularly important. Nothing would be more annoying than breaking a favourite bat through lack of care, and how foolish you would feel if you were run out by yards as a result of a missing spike! Before selecting equipment we strongly advise cricketers to contact a retailer who has a reputation for good service. Young players should ask senior players or coaches to recommend someone. Hard experience tells me that bargains are few and far between and most people get what they pay for.

Bats

There is no doubt that the majority of cricketers use too heavy a bat. Viv Richards and Clive Lloyd used to play with bats that is too heavy to life by others, let alone hit the ball with. A reasonable test for the weight of a bat is that it should be such that a batsman can easily manage a high and correct backlift using the top hand only (i.e. left hand for a right-handed batsman). Size is also an important consideration as is the length of the handle. I would never recommend the use of a long handle without a very careful assessment. Control of the bat is everything in good batsmanship and yet in general it is not given anything like the consideration it warrants.

Bats should be cared for by regular cleaning, using fine sandpaper as necessary and a light smear of bat or linseed oil as a preservative. Avoid oiling the splice, but oil the back of the bat when new as a seal against moisture. Repair edge cracks with a good quality glue and cover with adhesive tape. Make certain the grip is firm and in good condition—this is an essential. Break a bat in by bouncing a good quality leather ball on the hitting area until it has lost its initial softness and acquired a firm but resilient surface.

Unless one is in the millionaire class, be realistic in purchasing a bat. If playing regularly on bad wickets and having to hit cheap, two, or even one-piece "hard" balls, why go to the expense of buying the highest quality "soft" bat—which these days can be extremely expensive. There are excellent bats around made especially for the harder conditions that many clubs and school players have to endure. Do not scoff at a vellum covered bat; providing they are not too heavy they can give excellent service. If, however, it is a special occasion and a favourite relation insists on buying the bat, take time and select the bat with "feel" and balance. We were once advised by a fine Australian batsman, Jock Livingston, that an open grain (six to eight grains) gives the best performance, whilst a close grain bat wears the best but willow is a natural product and hard and fast rules cannot be made. Jock, an expert in the trade, suggests that one should think of selecting a bat just as you would a pair of shoes.

Protective equipment

When talking of protective equipment we always reminded of that great character and cricketer, Brian Close, then remember the doubtful pleasure of watching him face a fearsome West Indian pace attack at Old Trafford in the late '70's. On a number of occasions he unnecessarily let fast short-pitched deliveries hit him in the chest and ribs, taking great care not to rub the spot that was obviously causing him great pain. We admired his bravery, but it certainly could not have had the effect of convincing the batsmen due to follow him that the bowling was easy. It is important to wear the protection necessary for the conditions if you are to acquire the confidence necessary to play the game.

Firstly, every cricketer should wear an athletic

support with a pocket that will contain a protector or "box" as we call it. I see no reason why fielders in close catching positions or on bumpy outfields should not be so equipped. In many instances they are more likely to be hit than a batsman or wicket-keeper. A thigh pad may also be worn by batsmen to save unnecessary bruising.

The item of protective equipment that causes most discussion is the helmet, and whether or not it should be worn on all occasions. It is a matter for the individual, but youngsters may be guided by their mentors. Expense is a factor as helmets are very expensive. If they are available and there is obvious risk, would advocate their use, especially when they may give that vital spark of confidence to a young player. I am not sure that I agree with their use in the field however, as I believe that those in charge of the game should not allow youngsters to field in ridiculous "suicide" positions. One of these days a young cricketer is going to be seriously hurt, whether he is wearing a helmet or not, and then maybe stronger action will be taken.

Pads, of course, are our next line of defence against physical hurt. There are many designs. Make sure to select light pads and, if necessary, cut off the loose ends of the leather straps. Batting gloves are a necessity and care must be taken in their selection, mainly to make certain that they are comfortable and allow complete control of the bat—which very often they do not. Avoid tight-fitting clothing—nothing can put you off your game more. If anything, selecting a size too big can be a bonus, especially after a cleaning or a wash. We can hardly classify caps and sweaters under the heading "Protective Equipment", although we have known a cap save a nasty bump or two and it can protect the eyes against the glare of the sun.

In the English climate sweaters are an essential part of any cricketer's clothing. Under some circumstances a thick woollen sweater will protect you from more than the cold if you happen to be batting against a very fast bowler. An under-vest is also very useful in preventing stiffness and consequent injury after perspiring.

Footwear

There are so many different styles, selection of any one of them is difficult. Be sure that footwear is comfortable and allows for the wearing of thick woollen socks. Good quality footwear is a wise investment. Spiked boots are a must for most grounds and bowlers of any pace need to use them. Rubber soled footwear is only suitable for dry conditions, but an essential for indoor cricket.

Finally, remember to store your equipment properly, in clean conditions, particularly during the close season, and when the next match comes along you will have given yourself a better chance of enjoying the success your hard work has earned.

5

FIELDING

If there is one aspect of cricket that has changed in recent years, it is fielding. Now it is just as, if not more aggressive, than batting and bowling. Players are fitter than they have ever been; in fact, fielding at its best is now a spectator sport in itself. Players specialise in particular fielding positions, even differentiating between first and second slip, mid-wicket and mid-on. Without question, a successful team must be a good fielding side and practise together, as would a soccer or rugby team. A good fielding side somehow dominates the batsmen and makes ordinary bowling good and good bowling very good, as bowlers are encouraged, even "lifted", to give of their very best. Captains who study bowling tactics and field placing in depth are no longer in the minority and as a result, the tactical battle adds greatly to the interest in the game. "Catches win matches" is a saying that is proven time and again.

Ground fielding

Ground fielding may be logically divided into defensive fielding and attacking fielding, which, in turn, may also be divided into which, in turn, may also either intercepting or retrieving. Timing and judgment are a fielder's natural assets when coupled with the physical prowess to run fast, and throw with strength and accuracy. When the instant opportunity for a run-out occurs, the ability to keep cool under the pressure is also an asset worth having, although this can apply in any part of the game. Some cricketers are born with the unique ability to pick up and throw the ball when off balance. Obviously gifts like this must be undisturbed and, in fact, cultivated. The best ground fielders only show themselves in their true colours when a run-out situation occurs.

Defensive interception

This type of fielding can apply at any time, once it is absolutely certain that through its application a further run is not taken; neither is an opportunity of a run-out missed. There can only really be one defensive fielding technique and that is the Long Barrier. This position is concerned with safely intercepting and stopping the ball as efficiently as possible and then moving just as efficiently into a sound throwing position. There is no reason why a run-out should not be achieved from this position with a good throw.

When possible, the fielder moves into the line of the ball moving right, if be is a right-handed thrower. The riot foot is at right angles and behind the line of the ball, as the left knee bends fully to the ground just in front of the right heel. This presents a "long barrier" to the ball. The eyes watch the ball right into the hands, which are close together, fingers pointing down and just touching the ground. If the fielder has to move left and is a right-handed thrower, he still makes the barrier, only in this case dropping on to the right knee. From this position he takes one pace, pivoting on the right foot to achieve the throwing position.

Attacking interception

The one-handed pickup and throw from close in requires the fielder to move face-on to the line of the ball throughout the action. The throwing arm is drawn back only sufficiently to ensure the necessary speed of the ball through the air. From the longer distances, the thrower is looking for a two-handed pick-up, a good sideways position and a shoulder-level throw. Note the trailing foot in the classic position for giving balance whilst picking up the ball. When speed is the main essential, and if the fielder has the ability, a one-handed natural pickup and shoulder-level throw can be a winner.

Retrieving

Retrieving will nearly always be carried out at top speed and consequently must come under the heading of attacking fielding. The pick-up and throw on the turn is ideal for the close catcher looking for a run-out from the infield. For example, an edged ball, half-stopped by a slip fielder, can provide the ideal run-out from a fast pickup and throw on the turn. The throw must be made as the fielder is turning and jumping. The chase and retrieve from longer distances can be achieved by turning directly from the pick-up unless the ball is moving quickly. In this case the fielder's momentum normally takes his body a stride or two past the pickup position and the turn and pivot are made as soon as a sideways position can be established. In retrieving generally, ensure that the ball is picked up immediately alongside the foot below the throwing hand. For the really long throw from a slowly moving ball in the outfield, a pickup just inside and against the opposite foot from the throwing side is worth perfecting, i.e. left foot for right-handed throwers. When making the long throw using this technique, really push from the pickup foot. This creates a momentum for the long accurate throw.

Throwing

Of all the cricket skills, good throwing is the one most readily appreciated by spectators, whether it be from the outfield or the infield. Probably the most exciting of all dismissals is a run-out achieved by inches after a great pickup and throw. Accuracy, resulting from good technique, is all important and in many instances is the main factor in a run-out, although an early release of the ball is important in surprising the batsman. Also where run-outs are concerned it is important for the fielder nearest to the stumps to receive the throw in such a position that he can quickly remove the bails if necessary. All throws must be "backed-up" by the nearest available fielder to prevent overthrows at both the bowler's and the wicket-keeper's ends. Nothing is more depressing than a fielding side giving away overthrows from bad throwing and backing-up. Team practice can make this aspect of fielding worth watching.

There are three main throwing positions:

1. The long vertical overarm throw for distance and accuracy.
2. The shoulder-level throw from the infield for speed.
3. When extreme speed of return is needed from the in-field, a one-handed pick-up is the most effective, followed by an underarm throw.

Checkpoints

1. Ensure that for both overarm and shoulder-level throws, the right foot (right-handed throwers) is at right angles to the line of throw.
2. The non-throwing front arm gives a direction to the throw, the eyes looking over the left shoulder at the target.
3. The throwing arm is taken fully back for the long throw, with the hand cocked, but for the quick early release throw, the arm is bent and the throwing hand not cocked quite so much. In some instances, for an early throw, all the movement is from the elbow with the body quite open.
4. Weight transfer from back to front leg is important to achieve throwing momentum.

Catching

Regardless of the position in which you are fielding, there are common essentials that mean success or failure in this most important part of the game. Just one good catch at a vital stage to dismiss a good batsman and the team can be inspired. One simple catch dropped can have the most depressing effect on a team. At the same time, everyone admires a trier and the fielder who makes a great effort to take a catch will always enjoy his cricket and give enjoyment to others.

The common essentials of good catching are:

1. Sustained concentration on every ball delivered.
2. Minimum movement of the head, at least until the ball is sighted.
3. Good balance.

4. Relaxed hands, slightly cupped with the palms facing the ball.
5. Only slightly flexed arms (almost straight) will enable the hands to adjust to the path of the ball more easily and allow the hands to give as the ball is caught. All these principles also apply to wicket-keeping.

The high catch

Mainly failing to the outfielder, taking the high catch presents a psychological problem, rather than any other. Sometimes the ball seems to be in the air for a long time. The secret is to consciously relax and do not move in any direction until you have sighted the ball. Once sighted, move into the line as quickly as possible. Establishing a good base is an important factor. Try to take the catch high, before the ball has passed the eyes. This allows the eyes to follow the ball into the hands and also allows the hands to "give". Of course, this is an ideal example.

There is an increasing tendency, particularly amongst overseas players, to take the high catch in the same way as the baseball or skim catch. That is, with fingers pointing up, with palms facing the ball. This method is having a much higher success rate than the traditional high catching method. It is therefore important to acquire this technique.

Close catching

It is in the close catching positions that matches really are won and lost. Together with the wicket-keeper, the close catchers have more opportunities of dismissing early batsmen than any of the other forms of dismissal put together. The close catching positions are those that really do allow for the brilliant and inspiring effort. In general, players do not practise anything like enough to achieve the standards that are possible.

The three essentials of close catching are:

1. Establish a crouching position, equally balanced on the balls of the feet. The distance between the feet is important shoulder width is about right.
2. Concentration and the readiness to go for anything, preferably with two hands, but with one hand if necessary.
3. Close catchers should take care not to cover each other's territory. Staggered positions maximise the possibility of catches.

The fat trajectory or skim catch

Fielders in the covers and mid-wicket, midoff and mid-on, not to mention the close catchers, are likely to get a catch coming to them at an awkward chest or head height. These catches should be taken by simply inverting the hands, pointing the fingers upwards, but continuing to present the palms to the ball. This is sometimes known as the "baseball catch" and is a most effective method of catching a ball. In fact, it is the only way of catching a flat trajectory ball between chest and head height without jumping, which, more often than not, there isn't time for anyway.

Close catching positions

First slip

A highly specialised position, usually occupied by the best catcher available, as apart from the wicket-keeper, most catches are likely to go to first slip. It is good practice in this position to concentrate on watching the ball all the time, from the bowler's hand to the point when the batsman has played the stroke. First slip must remain still until the stroke has been played.

Second and third slips

These positions need all the qualities of the first slip. Most regulars in these positions watch the outside edge of the bat, rather than the ball, when awaiting the possibility of a catch. To avoid clashing when moving sideways for a catch, slip fielders should stagger their positions. Along with gully, second and third slips are probably the most difficult of the catching positions to occupy, as most catches come off a hard edge at high speed and very often the ball is spinning as a result of a mistimed attacking stroke.

Gully

A brave position and one which can cause uncertainty as to where to stand. Gully must be in the normal position to take the hard edge and bat shoulder catch. If he catches a full-blooded slash, that must be a bonus. On occasions, and for certain batsmen, gully can drop back a yard or two, with the special intention of trying to catch the slash or slightly mishit square-cut or cover drive. On no account must gully anticipate a catch. Concentrate on watching the bat. Experienced gully fielders are also aware of a batsman's foot movements.

Silly point, silly mid-off and mid-on

These positions are only utilised in exceptional circumstances. That is, for a new batsman, or when the fielding team have runs to spare and are trying to put pressure on a batsman. Silly positions are also utilised against defensive tail-end batsmen, or even to tempt a batsman into playing an unaccustomed stroke. Those occupying these positions should be ready to take evasive action at the slightest sign of danger. Keep your eye on the ball and do not turn your back on a stroke. Be aware that a ball hit against the spin will tend to go UP. This is a fact not utilised to the degree that it might be.

Lrg-slip

This position is very similar to first slip, only catches will generally come from the inside edge or even the face of the bat. Leg-slips are usually specialists in the leg-side close catching positions.

Short-legs—Forward and backward

Again, these positions are for the fearless. Short-leg fielders need to be brave, but not reckless. At the slightest hint of danger, evasive action should be taken. Short-legs are positioned normally for bat and pad catches, not full-blooded hits. The best short-leg fielders are crouched and poised on the balls of the feet, ready to move forward towards the bat. Hair trigger reflexes are needed in these positions.

Short mid-on, short mid-wicket, short mid-off and short extra

These are not quite close catching positions, but neither do they come under the heading of the infield. Positioned mainly for the mishit drive, with or against the spin, catches taken in these positions can leave the hands very warm. These positions are a great nuisance value and can also persuade a batsman to go for the really big hit, sometimes to his cost.

The In-field

Fielders in these positions need to be very quick off the mark, as it is their job to cut off the singles and fours, pressurising the batsman into making more vigorous and risky strokes. All in-fielders give themselves a few yards to walk in towards the batsman as the bowler commences his runup. This puts them on their toes ready to move quickly in any direction. In-fielders, if they are to err in positioning themselves, should do so to benefit their "strong" side. A common fault with infielders is to move in too close towards the batsman. That is, being too intent on saving the single but in fact failing to save the four.

Cover point

This position is usually occupied by the best ground fielder in the team. On a good pitch it is the busiest position and a good cover point can save hundreds of runs in a season. Lots of practice is essential, moving both to left and right. Cover point, together with mid-wicket, probably run out more batsmen than all the other positions on the field together. It is essential, therefore, that the ball can be picked up equally well with either hand, whilst running at speed. The ability to release the ball early, sometimes when off balance, is a great asset. A fast and accurate throw, if necessary underarm, complete a picture that makes cover point a vital position in any team. Mishit drives very often result in cover point having to take the awkward head-high skim or flat trajectory catch. Be prepared for this type of catch swinging a little in the air as a result of the "sliced" stroke.

Extra-cover

This position is well described in that more often than not it is a reinforcement or even a seal to the off-side field. All the qualities of a cover point are needed.

Mid-off and mid-on

Over the years both these positions have been underrated in their usefulness. They have tended to be "rest" positions for bowlers, or the captain's position, from which communications with the bowler are more easily accomplished. It is true that they are ideal for a captain, but, in fact, both positions are just as important to the in-fielding role of cutting off the singles. Batsmen, early in their innings particularly, are looking to push a single wide of mid-on or mid-off and, of course, this is when they are at their most vulnerable. Both positions are likely to be the recipients of hard-hit drives and catches. It is perhaps worth mentioning that when a fast bowler is in operation, the wide mid-on, very often the only fielder in front of the wicket on the leg-side, is in a key position.

Mid-wicket

As with cover point on the off-side of the wicket, mid-wicket is, perhaps, the busiest position on the leg-side, needing all the qualities of a cover point with, perhaps, the extra resilience in the, hands to catch a full-blooded pull stroke. Mid-wicket, together with cover point, may be allowed the luxury of anticipation occasionally, as they can very often see the batsman directing a stroke to steal a single.

Square-leg

Whilst this position should not be over-employed if the bowlers are doing their job, square-leg needs to have courage above all else. It is square-leg who has the task of not only cutting off the single, but stopping or catching the result of a long hop or leg-side full toss. It is very difficult to pick up the line and speed of the ball from a position square with the wicket at the best of times. When hit with full power, it can be impossible -- nearly! Square-leg is also in the awkward position of being the person the bowler mostly likes to think has wandered out of position. This, of course, is to cover his own embarrassment when bowling badly. Captains should be sympathetic to square-legs!

Short third-man

Another underrated position, from which a surprising number of run-outs are made. Fielders and captains need to carefully assess the conditions of the ground and the pitch before finally establishing the exact position that short third-man should field for any bowler. Short third needs special attention and experience counts for much. Invariably in dry conditions the ball will swerve at speed along the ground, particularly from the slightly mishit square-cut and as can be imagined, this can be most disconcerting when running quickly on to the ball. The swerve, fortunately, is always in the same direction, from square to fine, and therefore can be allowed for.

The out-field

The out-fielder may be defined as the fielder who, because of his position in the field, must accept the single, but no other scoring figure. The outfielder's main job is to dissuade the batsman from taking the extra run and if he does, give him a "run for his money". There can be no such thing as an easy catch in the outfield. Early positioning is essential, both in stopping the ball or making a catch. Out-fielders need to practise as much as anyone. Good throwing can give them their share of run-outs. Out-fielders must avoid the temptation to vary their position, particularly in walking in away from the boundary edge. It is much easier to make ground towards a catch, as against having to turn and attempt the catch coming over your shoulder. At the same time, the outfielder may need to establish a position well in from the boundary edge, when that boundary is a particularly long one. Common sense will prevail, but it must be disheartening for an outfielder to see a ball hit over his head and bounce inside the boundary. The outfielder or boundary fielder, as the position was once described, should be a very fast runner. Unfortunately, too often the position becomes a home for the tired fast bowler, or should say it did, as nowadays, with top-class fielding in all departments being an essential for good teams, fast bowlers are looking to become specialist close fielders for obvious reasons.

Wicket-keeping

There is a saying that wicket-keepers are born and not made. This may be true of the great wicket-keepers, but there is no doubt that the acquiring of sound techniques through hard practice can go a long way towards helping any enthusiastic young wicket-keeper to reach a very high standard of performance. There is no such thing as a bad wicket-keeper, at least not for very long, as he would be such a liability to the team as to make it an embarrassment for all and particularly the player concerned. This does not mean that a wicket-keeper cannot have a bad match occasionally. They all do, but somehow seem to bounce back and continue to enjoy their very full part in the game. A natural ability to catch the ball is a great asset to the aspiring wicket-keeper, as is the mobility achieved through a high level of physical fitness. A sense of humour is also of great benefit to the wicket-keeper in his position at the "centre of things". He can so often lift the team when the game is going against them and even afterwards in the dressing-room, he can play his part.

Equipment

Wicket-keeping equipment plays a much more important role in performance than is generally realised, particularly in so far as the gloves are concerned. Most of the wicket-keeper's equipment can be compared to that of the batsman's, with the exception of the wicket-keeping gloves and inners.

Gloves are probably the single item that can reduce a Test Match wicket-keeper to the lowest possible level, if they are not properly selected and cared for. We have often seen a young school wicket-keeper being given the job of catching the ball in a pair of something resembling boards rather than gloves. After a winter in cold storage, it is, of course, not surprising that they are not in the best condition, if they have not been prepared for the task ahead. It is important that the main gloves should be large enough to comfortably house inner gloved hands and still allow room to easily remove the glove from the throwing hand, if necessary. Both gloves, when new, should be lightly "hammered" in the palm with the bottom of a bat to develop the catching "cup". This should also be implemented by a lot of simple catching practice. The surface of the palm should be faced with soft pimpled rubber. Take care to replace this surface from time to time as it tends to become smooth and worn. Keep both gloves pliable, using leather dressing on the backs and cuffs. Too much packing in the palm of the gloves can result in a lack of "feel" when taking the ball. As in all equipment, lightness is vital for the speed of movement required by the hands. Inner gloves, preferably chamois, although cotton is as good, if not as durable, are an essential and sometimes an under-considered part of the wicket-keeper's gear. Many 'keepers bind the top finger joints with surgical tape over the inner gloves to create a finger stall that fits comfortably into the fingers of the main glove. If the inner gloves are not elasticated at the wrist, it is good practice to use a not too tight elastic band to give the compactness that will enable the main glove to be removed easily. Some wicket-keepers wet their chamois inners from habit—but the main reason for wetting the inners is to remove stiffness from the material usually caused from perspiration in their last outing. Other special points relating to wicket-keeping equipment are:

1. Do not use too long a spike in your cricket boots. They do tend to stick in the turf when turning or pivoting and this can easily be the cause of knee and ankle injuries.

2. A cap can be a useful means of focusing the eyes on the bowler's hand. It can also be a focal point for outfielders. The wicket-keeper can sometimes get "lost" amongst the close fielders when an outfielder is throwing from the boundary.

3. Make sure that you have the lightest of pads, with the ends of the straps cut neatly after fastening.

Stance

The normal position favoured by wicket-keepers is the squatting position, the weight equally on the balls of both feet, spaced comfortably apart. The seat is well down, the knees well bent and the hands are close together, resting between the legs with the tips of the fingers touching the ground and the palms open and facing the bowler. The chin is well up from the chest, with the eyes level in all planes.

Position

Standing up to the wicket, it is important for the wicket-keeper to be comfortable and to be in such a position relative to the batsman that the delivery of the ball can be easily seen. The inside foot should be no more than half a pace from the stumps when in position. Generally, the position of the inside foot will be in line with the off-stump.

When standing back from the wicket to the faster bowlers, a minority of wicket-keepers adopt a crouching, rather than a squatting stance. This resembles a slip fielder's stance, with, perhaps, more bend in the knees and hips. This stance is possibly useful to the less mobile keeper, enabling him to cover a wider range of sideways movements. The position of the wicket-keeper is the same, whether in the squatting or crouching stance. Again, when standing back, the wicket-keeper should have a clear view of the delivery of the ball, taking care not to stand so wide of the off-stump that he cannot easily take the ball going just down the leg-side.

One of the most common mistakes made by a wicket-keeper is in standing too close to the stumps when standing back. Sometimes called "standing in no man's land", this is a fault that occurs at the highest levels. Equally, the wicket-keeper should not stand too far back, thereby allowing the ball, and a possible catch, to bounce before reaching the hands. The ideal "take" for the normally paced delivery is between knee and waist height, letting the hands "ride" or "give" with the ball from a hands forward position, as the ball drops in its trajectory. Correctly setting this standing back position as early in the innings as possible, certainly within a few deliveries, is very important, as the close fielders (slips and short-legs) take their positions from the wicket-keeper.

Taking the ball

Having established a good stance and position, the next consideration by the wicket-keeper must be an intended taking of the ball, regardless of whether the batsman makes contact or not.

Standing back

1. Move into your stance position late, rather than early and avoid getting "set".
2. Do not move until the ball has been sighted leaving the bowler's hand. Only the very experienced wicket-keeper should anticipate any particular action, whether it be by batsman or bowler and even then, it is something to be guarded against.
3. Most catches come on the off-side of the wicket, therefore avoid getting wrong-footed by a ball pitched on the wickets. Think off-side, if anything.
4. Discuss tactics with your captain and the close catchers alongside you. Decide whether or not you wish first slip or first leg-slip to stand wide, giving you the opportunity of going for every possible catch. Remember, two hands are better than one and that one hand is better than none.

5. Look to getting behind the line of the ball, but be ready to sway off line if the ball comes to you at an awkward height.

6. After taking the ball, look to giving a quick easy catch to a nearby fielder, so that in turn, he can transfer it back to the bowler quickly.

Standing up to the wicket

1. As when standing back, move into you stance late, rather than early, to avoid getting "set".

2. Take extra care not to move too early. That is, be certain that you have picked up the trajectory and line of the ball before moving and then move quickly!

3. Come up with the bounce of the ball, not before.

4. Try to ignore any movement of the batsman and consider every ball to be yours. 5. Get behind the line of the ball, particularly when it is over-pitched. Be ready to move off the line of the short-pitched or good length delivery. This will enable you to "ride" with the ball if it lifts off a length or bounces higher or lower than expected.

6. Prepare to take the ball with the arms almost straight and relaxed. This allows the elbows to bend with the take. This is particularly so when taking the ball on the leg-side. Keep the elbows free from the body.

7. Avoid jumping or moving up and down as you move sideways, either to the off or leg. Try to keep the eyes moving in one plane.

8. Do not move the outside foot back, unless the ball

lifts, otherwise you will be taken out of range of the stumps.

9. Look to keeping the weight on the foot nearest to the wicket as you take the ball. Keeping your "weight" towards the wicket as you take the ball greatly helps the speed at which you can break the wicket.

10. When the batsman is playing back, try to take the ball as close to the bat as possible. This greatly enhances the chances of catching a thick edge.

General wicket-keeping advice

1. Concentration is everything. Even concentrate on concentration!

2. Catch the ball naturally in terms of bias towards the right or left hand. For example, if the right hand predominates in the normal catching of the ball, let it—do not try to change this consciously in a match.

3. The wicket-keeper can greatly help the captain. He is generally in the best position to notice any possible faults in a batsman's techniques. He is the first to know when a bowler has lost his "zip". Perhaps, more than anything, he should know just how the pitch is behaving, whether or not the ball is moving and so on. Of course, the wicket-keeper must have some experience and knowledge of what he may be commenting upon and even then, he should only really volunteer the information on request, or if generally agreed on policy with the captain.

4. Sometimes it pays to stand up on a bad wicket,

restricting the batsman's movement considerably. Conversely, standing back on a good wicket can pay dividends.

5. Do not use your pads to stop the ball. Always try to take the ball in your gloves, no matter how awkward the bounce.

6. Always stay within striking distance of the stumps when taking returns from the field, again, no matter how awkward the bounce. Remember that most run-outs are split-second affairs and speed in breaking the wicket is the main factor.

7. Keep a cheerful demeanour all the time, no matter what the state of the game. You are the leader of the orchestra and nothing is worse for a team than to see their wicket-keeper "down in the dumps".

8. Keep yourself fit by regular training (see section on fitness). Squash is a marvellous game for wicket-keepers, as it encompasses nearly all the movements required when played hard.

9. Practice hard in taking the ball from the most awkward bounces.

6

LENGTH AND DIRECTION

Before becoming too involved in analysing the various cricket skills, it is important to understand certain concepts of the game that concern both batsman and bowler. Only through this knowledge will you be able to improve your technique on sound principles. Because of the abstract and comparatively complex nature of some of these concepts, over the years they have acquired a mystique that cricketers themselves delight in, when projecting their game to the outsider. Of course, the arguments that are brought forth are part of cricket's attraction, as in the end we all like to interpret the game in our own way. Nevertheless, tog loss over the mysteries of length, for example, would, I feel, be like starting to climb a mountain without a rope, or maybe learning to drive a car using only one gear, or some similar analogy.

Length

The word "length" "in cricket refers to the point at which the ball pitches in relation to the batsman when in his normal stance at the wicket. Fully understanding the meaning of a "good length" in all the circumstances you might encounter in a match is one of cricket's most difficult problems, applying equally, but for different reasons, to batsmen and bowlers.

A good length may be described as that length of delivery that causes the batsman most hesitation as to whether to play back or forward. To bowl a good length at will is the objective of every bowler. Many cricketers learn the meaning of a good length through hard experience. Others, who are few and far between, are born with the gift of ball sense that enables them to recognise a good length instinctively. Because of differences in physical makeup, speed of reaction and technical ability, what may be a good length to one batsman need not be to another. Similarly, a good length bowled by a slow bowler is different from that bowled by a quicker bowler if it is to achieve the same reaction from the batsman in terms of doubt as to whether to play back or forward. The prevailing atmospheric conditions, the state of the playing surface and even the condition of the ball, whether it be old or new, are important influences on what is a good length for a particular delivery. For example, when the ball is new and the atmosphere is heavy and conducive to the ball swinging, a good length is slightly nearer the batsman than it would otherwise be. On slower playing surfaces (pitches), a good length is again nearer to the batsman than it would be on a quicker surface.

Bounce

To start, one might say that bounce is to do with the speed of the playing surface a fast or a slow pitch, or wicket as it is often referred to. It is true that generally the faster the Playing surface the higher the bounce. This is not always the case, however, as bad or wet surfaces sometimes produce excessive bounce without them being Particularly fast. Again, the ball itself bounces differently as it becomes older. Also, Providing they deliver the ball with a high action, tall bowlers obviously achieve more bounce than those not so tall. Bounce can have many interpretations, but I am looking at it in the context of "length" and its relationship with batting, or more specifically, its effect on the batsman', decision to play forward or back. There is no doubt that the good batsman in planning his innings has, if Possible, taken the likely variations that influence bounce into consideration He will, knowing his own style of play, have some idea of how he will cope with high or low bounce. Invariably, the Most displeasing pitch on which a batsman can play is one on which bounce is variable from a constant length.

So to the main reason for this discourse; back or forward forward or back? When and how? Good batsmen are instinctive in their reactions, but a good batsman is a prepared batsman If anticipated bounce is low, look to play forward back, if the bounce is likely to be high. But what is high and low? High bounce may be interpreted by a batsman as that bounce of delivery that hits the bat splice or higher when playing normally forward to a good length ball. Low bounce may be interpreted as that bounce of delivery that would hit the batsman below knee height when playing normally back. Depending upon anticipated bounce and the style of batsman he is bowling to, a good length varies for each type of bowler. In general, the higher the bounce the nearer the batsman the attacking bowler will pitch the ball, looking to bring him forward and commit him to a stroke. If the batsman is known as a committed forward player in any case, the bowler will be more effective shortening his length a little and vice versa for the committed back Player.

Recognised names for length of delivery

Good length

As described previously, this is the length bowlers must be looking to pitch nearly every ball. Occasionally a bowler may deliberately try to bowl a yorker or a bouncer in an effort to surprise and therefore dismiss a batsman, An appreciation of a good length can be acquired to some degree by the recognition of what is not a good length, The following descriptions of various length deliveries will emphasise this point.

Long hop

A delivery that pitches approximately halfway down the pitch, slow enough for the batsman to consider it a gift. Can be hit hard anywhere in front of the wicket, but generally is pulled on the leg-side.

Short ball

Short bowling is bad bowling. Depending upon direction the batsman can play any one of the attacking back strokes to a short delivery on a good surface. Even on a bad Pitch the short ball can cost runs.

Short of a length

Pitching much nearer to the batsman than the long hop, or short ball, this delivery is, as its name implies, short of a good length. A defensive delivery on a good pitch, it can be a useful wicket-taker on a difficult pitch (when the ball is lifting or keeping low) for the faster bowlers.

Half volley

Pitching beyond a good length, this is the delivery that every batsman should be looking to hit hard just after it pitches—and yet when the ball is swinging and the batsman is not well set, it can be a wicket-taker through catches behind the wicket.

Yorker

Pitching approximately at the batsman's feet, the yorker is a very effective wicket taker (bowled) if delivered with a little extra pace. A surprise delivery that can easily become a full toss or half volley.

Full toss

Like the long hop, this delivery is looked upon by batsmen as a gift. Not pitching at all, the height at which the ball reaches the batsman can determine the stroke.

Bouncer

Much has been said and written about the bouncer. It pitches generally in a similar area to the long hop, but is delivered at an extremely fast pace. The ball pitches and lifts towards the batsman's chest and head.

Beamer

A head-high full toss. Under no circumstances should any bowler attempt to bowl this delivery, as it can be dangerous to the batsman.

The length of a delivery determines the stroke a batsman will attempt. If the correct stroke is played for the length bowled, a batsman will be likely to score and in most circumstances will certainly retain his wicket. If a batsman misjudges length and plays the incorrect stroke, it is likely that he will be dismissed.

In all the batting skills, care has been taken to ensure that the type of delivery for each stroke is clearly stated. Hence the importance of these notes.

Direction

Allied to good length and equally important is good direction. The ball should be directed either on or just outside the off-stump in most circumstances. In the same way that length is perhaps not considered deeply enough in cricket, neither is direction. There really is so much to consider, that understandably young players want to get on with bowling, hitting and catching the ball.

The basic requirement of good direction is to pitch the ball on a good length somewhere between the middle and just outside the off-stump, with the primary object of making the batsman play at the ball. This makes sense when considering that the more skilled batsmen are more often than not dismissed early in their innings through catches behind the wicket. However, the batsman will only have to play at the ball if he thinks that by not doing so, the ball may hit the wicket.

On good pitches, with little movement of the ball in the air or off the pitch, it is fair to assume that the ball will continue its line of initial direction before and after pitching, In which case, should the bowler deliver the ball from wide on the bowling crease, it is more likely to easily miss the wicket than if the delivery had been from close to the stumps, i.e. bad, rather than good direction. When conditions allow the ball to move considerably in the air (swing bowling) or off the pitch (spin bowling), the reverse situation applies in that to achieve good direction, that is make the batsman play at the ball, it can be necessary for the bowler to deliver the ball from wide rather than from close to the stumps. A little study will soon confirm that the bowler's delivery position at the crease will depend upon the anticipated movement of the ball, either off the pitch or through the air. Whilst variation will always be a keyword in good bowling, in most instances, and certainly when bowling at the better batsmen, the bowler will be looking to find a thin edge of the bat through the compromise of delivery position and anticipated movement of the ball.

A bowler is said to be bowling over the wicket if his bowling arm is on the side nearest the stumps on delivery. He is bowling round the wicket when his body comes between the stumps and his bowling arm on delivery. Generally, bowlers only bowl round the wicket when there is considerable movement of the ball in towards the batsman (i.e. off-spinners; right-arm inswing bowlers).

7

BOWLING

It has been said that the last bowler to be knighted was Sir Francis Drake! It is true that the bowler, no matter how successful he is, somehow does not quite excite the cricket loving public in the way that the great batsman does. Perhaps it is because the bowler, and in particular the fast bowler, takes on the role of villain, as, through his aggressive actions both physically and sometimes verbally, he intimidates both batsman and umpire. Perhaps it is the feeling of the batsman standing alone at the wicket, taking on all comers, that gives him the role of hero. Perhaps, and most likely, the artistry of the great batsman is more visible and consequently more easily appreciated than that of the bowler. Whichever, it is so, albeit through the wiles of the media, the image is charging to promote batsmen and fast bowlers equally as the heroes of cricket - and why not? There can be no doubt that recognition for a bowler is much harder to achieve physically, but in being so is more achievable, as effort replaces flair and becomes the catalyst which opens the door to any strong, determined and intelligent young player who has a yearning for the crowd's applause. Let no one think, however that it is anything like so easy as a few words and dreams can make it wound. Bowing is a grind; long hours of net bowling, of physical training, of disappointments galore when everything has been achieved but the catch that claims the wicket. Even then some indefinable something has to be added to the effort; could it be subtlety?

One aspect of bowling that has recently taken a turn for the better is its coaching. At one time, all the coach required from a bowler was good length and line. Batting was the main interest. Not so today. The coaching of bowling has been recognised as a key to success and I recommend a bowler as much as a batsman to look for good coaching and advice. I am convinced that the time is close when success ; in bowling will again be measured in overs per wicket and not runs per over.

Jack Mercer of Sussex's career spans over sixty years as a player, coach, umpire, scorer, magician (member of the Magic Circle) and raconteur supreme. He played in the golden age, perhaps the only man alive today who did. His advice on bowling is worth recall "Bowling is all about pitching the ball up to the bat, bringing the batsman forward". He also said to me: "When a bowler follows through looking over his bowling shoulder at the batsman, you can rely or him having bowled a good ball". Just of a great cricketer's thoughts. It shall add one word "planning". Plan your over, plan each ball, plan your net practice and if you are not approaching six foot tall and built like a tank, do not be disheartened. The best of bowling is for the spinner, the real artist, whose guile is essential to the future of the game.

The basics of bowling

In all instances, to simplify descriptions, it is assumed, unless otherwise stated, that a right-arm bowler is bowling over the wicket to a right-handed batsman. Of all the skills in cricket. The bowler always, or nearly always, has another chance, whereas the batsman can usually only make one mistake. Another feature of bowling is that we nearly all can do it, or like to think we can. This is true, up to a point, in that bowling appears to be that much simpler than batting, although I do not suppose such a comment will gain much support from bowlers. To practise batting, a bowler (of sorts) is needed. To practise bowling, a batsman is not absolutely necessary. Bowling is more physical than batting and whilst that does not make it simpler, the basic requirements are perhaps more easily defined. There are, in fact, only four the grip (of the ball), the run-up, the delivery and the follow-through. Of course, there are many variations on each of these basics to produce the different types of delivery, but these variations are refinements, not alterations, and take nothing away from the analysis of the basic structure of bowling that follows.

Comment

This is the grip from which variations can be made to give the type of delivery required. It is essentially a finger grip, rather than a palm grip.

Checkpoints

1. The first two fingers lie alongside the seam, easily apart.
2. The inside of the thumb lies on the seam, directly beneath the first two fingers.
3. The third finger rests lightly against the ball, simply acting as a support.

4. There is a noticeable gap at the vee of thumb and first finger.

Run-up

Whether a slow bowler or a fast bowler, the same principles apply. The object of the run-up is to enable the bowler to move into the delivery stride with the balance and the momentum necessary to consistently deliver the ball with the maximum desired effect. I have found the run-up to be a sadly neglected part of bowling instruction, analysis and practice.

Comment

Rhythm is the key to a good run-up and this is what the bowler must constantly be trying to obtain. In practice, it is not uncommon for the coach to call out the timing. Check the length of your run-up and mark it clearly. Too short a run-up can be just as bad as too long a run-up. Time spent on establishing the right length of run-up to give you rhythm is time well spent.

Checkpoints

1. Face the batsman; start slowly, gradually lengthening your stride and increasing your speed. Watch the batsman closely, progressively concentrating on the spot where you wish the ball to land.
2. Running at a very slight angle to the wicket may help you to "bound" into the delivery stride. That is, jump forward and high enough to enable you to turn fully sideways. Land with your right foot (for right-handed bowlers) parallel to the crease.

Delivery

This is the heart of the bowling action and is, without

doubt, the major key to success in bowling. Take particular note of the "bound" which may be described as the link between the run-up and the delivery. As the run-up takes you into the bound and hence the delivery stride, be conscious that you are leaning back away from the batsman. This position enables the fast bowler to get maximum momentum through the delivery stride. Remember that up to twenty per cent of the speed of the ball as it leaves the bowler's hand comes from the speed of movement through the delivery stride.

As you land from the bound, you are about to go through what is called the "coil" position. At this position, the front foot is raised, the knees flexed, the front arm high, but not in such a position as to block the bowler's view. The eyes look over the front shoulder at the point where you wish to pitch the ball. Some experienced bowlers develop a personal point of aim to suit themselves. I he bowling hand is held up to the chest, just below the chin, When viewed by the batsman, the back is slightly arched to achieve maximum height. When landing in the coil position, the lean away from the batsman is still very evident.

Still in a good sideways position, the delivery stride (longer for the fast bowler; shorter for the slow bowler) is commenced. The length of the stride is important in that too short a stride will cause a lessening of the body action, while too long a stride can not only lose height in the delivery, but slow down the delivery stride itself. Note the open palm facing the batsman and the delayed action of the bowling hand.

As the bowler comes through the delivery stride, the front shoulder guides the weight on to the left leg, flexed at the knee to take the impact created by the faster bowler, but braced following the shorter delivery stride of the slower bowler. When bowling fast, the wrist is cocked back to give maximum acceleration of the ball as it is released. The fast bowler's delivery stride is completed with the front foot landing virtually in line with the back foot when viewed by the batsman. For the slower bowler, with the shorter stride, the front foot lands slightly across the body. A high delivery position is basic, but it can be varied slightly, as required by the bowler's intention. The seam should be vertical at the point of release.

Follow-through

A good follow-through is a must for all successful bowlers. The first follow-through stride is towards the batsman. The right knee leads the follow-through close past the left, without any splaying. The eyes are still looking down the pitch over the bowling shoulder. The bowling arm has cut closely past the left side and the left arm is taken vigorously through and well back, past the hip. Continue to decelerate naturally, still running as straight as possible down the pitch, bearing in mind that the bowler is not allowed to run on the pitch more than four feet past the bowling crease and one foot either side of the middle stump. Check this part of your follow-through in practice.

Pace bowling

Fast bowling

The genuine fast bowler is a rarity indeed and to see the best in full cry is a special treat. Every young cricketer wants to be a fast bowler, but few have the physical gifts required. It is important to recognise the boy who can bowl fast for his age and, if possible, steer him carefully in those teenage years when so many are lost through lack of guidance.

The basics laid down in the previous pages cover nearly all the requirements of the fast bowler's action. Variations from pure speed such as swing and cut, can be added later, as can variation in pace and angle of attack. Proper fitness training, incorporating strength training routines, are a must for the keen young pace bowler. Good habits learned early will stand you in good stead later. For the young bowler who really has the potential to bowl fast, I should make that in itself the priority, rather than gear your action or thinking to swing or cut at too early a stage. Length and direction are important, of course, but again "think fast" first. Having said this, training should be tempered by good sense in taking care not to bowl for too long or trying to bowl too fast, especially when you are young and still growing.

Medium

Whilst the fast bowler is initially likely to concentrate on speed only, developing swing and other variations as a secondary consideration, the medium-paced bowler must concentrate on becoming an expert in one or more of the variations that should be a part of the medium-pacer's repertoire.

There are three main classifications of medium-pace which can be mixed, depending upon the bowler's ability. They are swing bowling (in and outswing), seam bowling, wherein the bowler relies on a very precise delivery of the ball to pitch on the vertical seam, and two types of cutter (off and leg), wherein the bowler drags his finger across the ball at delivery, imparting a degree of off or leg spin.

Swing bowling

Before looking at the action that produces swing or swerve in the air, it is important to realise why the cricket ball swings as compared to say the table tennis or golf ball. Since the seam was first introduced as a feature of the cricket ball there has been little variation in its construction. In fact, the seam is simply a result of sewing together the leather outer casing of the cricket ball. The stitches holding the outer casing together stand up from the general surface of the ball in such a way as to create a ridge around the circumference of the ball. By projecting the ball through the air in one way or another, the atmosphere, either dense or thin, exerts forces on the ridge, causing the ball to drift in one direction or another. Over the years bowlers have acquired the art of releasing the ball very accurately and presenting the ridge or seam (as we shall call it) to the prevailing conditions in such a way as to obtain maximum side forces. Consequently, the longer the ball is in the air, the more it will swing. This is not the advantage it may first appear as, more often than not, we look for subtle swing rather than a too obvious swing. Bowlers should experiment by varying the position of the seam slightly. Variations in conditions cause the ball to swing more or less. Variations in pace cause the ball to swing earlier or later in its flight. If at least one side of the ball is kept smooth or even shiny, the seam will have greater effect due to the difference in air pressure on the smooth side, as against the rough side of the ball.

The outswinger swings in the air towards the slips, when bowled to a right-handed batsman. The inswinger swings in the air from off to leg, when bowled to a right-handed batsman.

The outswinger

The grip and action

The grip varies from the basic, in that whilst the seam is vertical on delivery, it is angled towards the slips (First or Second), The inside of the thumb lies against the edge of the seam. At the moment of release, the fingers should be behind the ball with the wrist firm. This action can cause a slow backward rotation of the ball that helps steady the seam for maximum swing towards the slips.

Comment

When bowling to a right-handed batsman, the outswing bowler should be pitching the ball on a full length in line with the off-stump or just outside, attempting to bring the batsman forward.

Checkpoints

1. Delivering the ball from close to the wicket (i.e. bowling between wicket and wicket) increases the effect of the swing. If the ball is swinging a lot, the bowler can go wider on the crease to achieve the same result.

2. Angling the wrist rather than the arm towards the slips helps to conceal the action from the batsman, and in this way the arm can be kept higher.

3. Stay sideways as long as possible during delivery. Follow through vigorously, the bowling arm swinging across the body.

The Inswinger

The grip and action

The grip varies from the basic in that whilst the seam is vertical, it is angled towards fine-leg. The ball of the thumb is placed flat against the middle of the seam, At the moment of release, again, the fingers should be behind the ball with the wrist firm.

Comment

The inswing bowler should be pitching the ball on a full length on the off-stump, bringing the batsman forward. If the ball is swinging a lot, it can be pitched up to a foot outside the off-stump, the bowler looking for the batsman's "gate".

Checkpoints

1. In the delivery stride, the body opens much more for the inswinger, the back foot pointing more towards the batsman.
2. The arm should be high and the bowler should have the feeling of pushing the ball on its way.
3. The bowling arm follows through a little less vigorously than in the outswinger and may finish between right hip and wicket, rather than across the body.

Seam bowling

For the seam bowler to be effective, the seam must project well clear of the surface of the ball. The skill of the seam bowler lies in the ability to constantly pitch the ball on the vertical seam, allowing the pitch, providing it is receptive, to deviate the ball in one direction or another.

The grip for seam bowling is exactly as described under the heading "The Basic Grip". The wrist position is very important at the point of release, as it may have to be inclined very slightly one way or another to obtain the desired seaming effect. Seam bowling is limited in application, as to be really effective, a "green" pitch is required. That is, a well grassed, slightly damp pitch, which acts as a resilient cushion to the seam. A good swing bowler can often use the seam very effectively. The natural finger action on the ball is a slight dragging back of the two top fingers at the instant of release. This has a stabilising effect on the ball. The good seam bowler relies heavily on variation in pace and extreme accuracy.

Cutters

The cutter is a useful variation for the swing bowler, although in the right conditions it can be the main striking force, rather than a variation. A soft drying pitch is the ideal surface with the dusty pitch of variable bounce coming a close second. The fingers cut or drag down the side of the ball, causing clockwise or anti-clockwise spin. Bowled at a faster pace than the spinner, the cutter's imparted spin has a lesser effect in terms of deviation. The following technical descriptions note the first or second finger using the seam as a wedge to cut the ball. Some bowlers bowl cutters with a normal spinner's grip, but in doing so, cannot generate pace to the same degree.

Grip

The first finger is the main spinning finger. The top joint of this finger crosses the seam. The second or middle finger takes up a similar position, the two fingers being spread as widely as is comfortably possible, to give the maximum spinning leverage. The third finger curls lightly along the seam, acting together with the base of the thumb simply as a support. The thumb takes no part in the spinning of the ball. Again, the ball must be held only in the fingers and away from the palm.

Comment

I firmly believe that to become a good spin bowler, you must have the ability to really spin the ball, even if you do not always use that ability. In fact, once a batsman knows you can spin the ball a lot, he will always have it in his mind and may subconsciously play for the spin whether it is there or not.

Checkpoints

1. The action is basic in that it is classically sideways, with the bowling arm taking a full swing into a high delivery.
2. The ball is delivered against a braced left leg, the delivery stride being slightly across the crease and short enough for the bowler to "stand tall".
3. The spinning action is vigorous, simulating the right hand "opening of a door" and dragging the seam in a clockwise direction.
4. A full follow-through is as essential to the off-spin bowler as it is to the fast bowler, the right arm cutting across the body past the left hip.

The floater

The joker in the off-spinner's pack is the floater. The best exponents of this delivery, in particular the legendary Jim Laker, have the ability to make it appear just like an off-spinner to the batsman. In fact, as the ball floats towards the slips, it can have the same effect as a googly by completely deceiving the batsman who can so easily play for the off-spin,

Grip

Very similar to the alternative off-spin grip but with the thumb located behind the ball on delivery.

Comment

This is an action that should be experimented with in an effort to deceive the batsman. Instead of the spinning finger dragging the seam in a clockwise direction, it pushes the ball towards the slips. A variation on the floater lets the first finger slide round and under the ball as it leaves the hand, making the delivery look even more like an off-spinner.

The Top-spinner

Another useful wrist-spin variation, in which significant forward spin is imparted to the ball, giving the impression that it gathers speed on pitching. One might say that there can be no such a delivery as a top-spinner, in that unless it is bowled with perfect forward spin only, there must always be some degree of leg or off-spin on the ball. However, it is worth allowing the definition "top-spin", bearing in mind that the bowler should be looking for differences between the various wrist-spin deliveries. As in the googly, there are two types of top-spinner. In the high bowling action, the wrist bends and drops and the ball is slipped out of the back of the hand over extended fingers. It is almost a googly action, but the wrist has not turned so far. This may be called the googly top-spinner. The more effective top-spinner is bowled from a lower arm action in just the same way as a genuine leg-break. The difference is that the wrist is turned so that the seam points straight down the pitch and the third finger applies the strong over-spin.

Spin variations

I first became interested in the possibilities of spinning the ball in different directions and with different actions when keeping wicket to the great Australian spin bowler George Tribe, and more recently after discussing the art with the well-known Australian coach, Peter Philpott, and today's leading practitioner, Abdul Qadir. Peter is probably the supreme authority on the subject as wrist-spin is a subject on which Australians specialise, although currently, it does not seem to be in favour with any country. Nevertheless, I am of the opinion that young cricketers in this country would benefit from developing an interest in this fascinating subject. Try using the grips that have already been described to simply toss the ball in the air.

Another great Australian cricketer and broadcaster, Richie Benaud, dominated Australian spin bowling in the fifties and sixties using a wide range of wrist-spin tactics. We believe he had great success with a backspin delivery that had the effect of keeping very low on pitching. Probably the most famous of the mystery deliveries was the flipper, which was perfected by three other Australian greats, Bruce Dooland, George Tribe and Cecil Pepper.

More experiment will be needed, but may have kindled some interest for some young cricketer somewhere. At least, it may start some readers asking questions. Finally, for all potential spin bowlers, remember that spin without flight is like bread without butter or, depending upon where you come from, fish without chips!

To recapitulate

1. An off-spinner is a delivery bowled by a right-handed (finger-spin) bowler, that turns from the off to the leg-side when bowled to a right-handed batsman.

2. A leg-spinner is a delivery bowled by a right-handed (wrist-spin) bowler, that turns from the leg to the off-side when bowled to a right-handed batsman.

3. A googly is a delivery bowled by a right-handed (wrist-spin) bowler, that turns from the off to leg-side when bowled to a right-handed batsman. The difference from the off-spinner is that the ball is released with a wrist-spin, rather than a finger-spin, action. One might say that the googly is an off-break bowled with a leg-break action.

4. Off and leg-cutters are the same in principle as the off-spinner and leg-spinner described above

5. An outswinger is a delivery that swings in the air from the leg to the off-side of the wicket.

6. An inswinger is a delivery that swings in the air from the off to the leg-side of the wicket.

Summary

It will be appreciated from the above that it is the batsman that determines the description. That is, the off-side and leg-side are dependent upon whether the batsman is right or left-handed. Leg-side to a right-handed batsman is the off-side to a left-handed batsman. Cricket is, indeed, a strange game, as we now have the situation that when a right-handed bowler bowls an off-spinner (off-breaks) to a left-handed batsman, whilst it is an off-spinner to all intents and purposes, it is, in fact, a leg-spinner to the left-handed batsman.

The left-arm bowler

Having looked briefly at the problems created by a left-handed batsman, the left-arm bowler, of necessity, must be clearly identified. The slow left-arm finger-spin bowler who delivers the ball with the same action as the right-handed off-spin bowler in fact bowls leg-breaks to a right-handed batsman (i.e. the ball spins in the opposite direction to the off-break). However, this type of bowler is not identified as a leg-break bowler. That title is reserved for the right-handed wrist-spinner. For purposes of identification, the slow left-arm finger-spin bowler is simply known as a slow left-arm bowler or a S.L.A. Generally, the slow left-arm bowler bowls round the wicket to the right-handed batsman, so that his natural spin forces the batsman to play at the ball.

We now consider the left-handed wrist-spin bowler. It is sure you will now appreciate that if this type of bowler delivers the ball with the same action as the right-handed wrist-spinner, the ball will spin in the opposite direction. That is, the leg-break will be an off-break to the right-handed batsman. The special name for this delivery is the "chinaman" and the reason for this, unfortunately, has got to be another story! A googly is a googly from whichever hand it is bowled. After these rather complex descriptions, we come to the medium and fast left-arm bowlers. In their case, it is glad to say that they are simply identified as medium or fast swing bowlers, depending upon which way they mainly swing the ball to the right-handed batsman. The left-handed pace bowler does, however, invariably bowl over the wicket to both right-handed and left-handed batsmen.

Bowling tactics

Flight

Flight is another subject that is not to the foremost in general cricket discussion and yet it has a significant bearing on slow bowling. A flighted delivery is one in which the ball is projected upwards from the bowler's hand, rather than downwards at the instant of delivery. We are sure that it will be appreciated that this presents another problem for a batsman in that he has to judge when the flighted delivery begins to descend. Only then can he begin to judge the length. Hence the expression sometimes heard on a radio or television commentary when a batsman is dismissed by a spin bowler, "he was beaten in the flight". A good spin bowler uses flight as a main weapon as he looks to produce the mishit drive from a batsman. A well flighted ball very often looks to the batsman as if it is going to carry further than it actually does, resulting in him trying to drive a good length delivery, thinking, initially, that he is hitting a half volley. The really high class slow bowler will even vary his flight by releasing the ball from different positions within the arc of his delivery. By letting the ball go early, rather than later, the ball will stay in the air longer, introducing yet another variation.

Variation in pace

Whatever individual quality or skill a bowler may bring to his art, subtle variation of pace remains the key to consistently reaching the highest standards of performance. Whilst this is an obvious weapon for the slow bowler especially when related to flight, lam sure it could be used to greater effect by the fast bowler, providing that the variation is subtle. It has certainly been the success factor with the best fast bowlers in recent years.

Angle of attack

Angle of attack is relative to direction and is mentioned briefly under that heading, but it should be realised that the different angles can be produced in different planes. A slight lowering of the arm, for example, will produce a slightly different angle for the batsman to consider.

Field placing

Field placing for individual bowlers is one of the most important aspects of good bowling and good captaincy. It is underrated as a means of winning matches and receives nothing like the study it deserves from most cricketers. Over the years, standard field placings for different types of bowlers have been evolved and generally they work quite well in standard conditions against standard batsmen. In recent years, Bill Frindall, Test Match scorer and statistician supreme, has presented these aspects of cricket in a most interesting way. Cricketers should be aware that field placing in general is an untapped source of interest and information, and hope they will be encouraged, as captains and bowlers, to experiment in improving their teams' results. A few pointers on field placing are included under the chapter on Captaincy. A general diagram, relating to the following specific diagrams, comes into the chapter on Fielding.

Field placings for different types of bowling

Fast/medium outswing

The diagram shows a typical field placing for the commencement of an innings on a firm wicket with some bounce. If the opening bowler is very fast, adjustments can be made as follows:

Third-man (3) can move to third slip (A); mid-off (6) can move to fourth slip (B) or square gully (C). In this case, cover point (5) should move straighter to (D).

Only the very best of fast bowlers are advised to bowl to this attacking field. Generally, the original field placings shown in the diagram (1--10) are very suitable. As soon as the shine goes off the ball, if there is no movement in the air, short square-leg (8) may be moved to field at (E).

Fast/medium inswing

If the opening bowler is very fast, adjustments can be made to the field as follows:

Third-man (2) may move to second slip (A) and mid-off (4) to gully (B). In this case, cover point (3) would move straighter. If, in the first few overs, a wicket had not fallen, second slip (A) would return to third-man (2). If the ball was only swinging a little, mid-wicket (6) could move to second slip (A), giving four on the leg-side, as against five. In this case, it may be good policy for short square-leg (7) to move out to square-leg (C).

Defensive

Medium-pace bowling

In most types of cricket, it is sometimes necessary to bowl defensively, or change from attack to defence for different batsmen etc. The diagram shows a typically defensive split field that requires extreme accuracy for it to be really effective, In cases where defence has to be carried to the extreme, positions (2), (4) and (7) can be positioned on the boundary edge. Even first slip (1) can retreat halfway to the boundary, occupying the position of fly-slip (A).

Off-spin

If the off-spinner wishes to direct his attack more at the middle and leg-stumps, extra-cover (4) would need to move to deep mid-wicket (A), in which case, cover point (3) would move straighter. When bowling on a turning pitch or attacking specifically, the following adjustments would need to be made to some degree:

Short fine-leg (9) would need to come in short, as would mid-wicket (7). Extra cover (4) would then need to be at deep mid-wicket (13) and point (2) would need to be at short mid-on (C). In some circumstances, it would be sound policy to move first slip (1) to the position of short third-man (D) allowing mid-off (5) to retreat to deep mid-off (E). In either case, cover point-would move much straighter, almost level with the bowler's wicket.

Leg-spin/googly

The diagram shows a typical field for a good wicket. Extra-cover may field on the boundary. If the ball begins to turn, short third-man may be moved to gully and extra-cover to short extra. Mid-wicket may be moved to forward short-leg. These moves would be made for a leg-spin bowler, only if he is extremely accurate, or if the batsman is defensive.

Slow Left-arm

The diagram shows what may be termed the classical old-fashioned field for the S.L.A. on a good wicket. In recent years, slow left-arm bowlers have bowled more at the wickets and have invariably positioned a fielder at the forward short square-leg position for the bat and pad catch.

Backward point moves to gully. Point moves squarer and closer. Extra-cover moves to short extra. Mid-wicket moves to short mid-on Mid-on may move to deep mid-on.

8

BATTING

Every batsman, young or old, talented or otherwise, must dream at some time of playing the ultimate innings, despatching the greatest bowlers to ail parts of the ground with a glittering display of strokes. In reality such innings rarely occur, but there is no reason why any batsman should not improve by adopting a more realistic approach to the game. How many batsmen, week in and week out, play beautifully until reaching double figures? Then, for some reason or another, they virtually change character and attempt to play strokes that are simply not on. In astonishing self-deceit, they resort to blaming the pitch, the umpire, the light, the bat, or even the "night before" for their lack of success. Maybe occasionally the bowler gets credit, but seldom does the batsman admit that he just cannot play the stroke that leads to his downfall. Perhaps it is likely that during a hard week's work, a glimpse of some great batsman on television has caused a "rush of blood" and the desire to smash the ball into another world and why not indeed. At a guess though, we think most of those who fall early in their innings would love another chance and next time they would play the stroke to perfection. That is, of course, after having practised some of the techniques of batting described in the following pages!

First things first and whilst you do not have to become an Olympic athlete, reasonable physical fitness is a must for any batsman worth his salt. The chapter on Fitness presents a simple range of training that should suit most requirements.

A problem confronting many cricketers is that they find themselves guided into styles of play and sections of the game to which they are not necessarily suited, either physically or mentally. Whenever you are learning a new technique, it should only be practised in the knowledge that it is achievable. Always assess your own capabilities. Are you mainly a front foot player or a back foot player? For some reason or other, it has always been fashionable for English batsmen to cultivate the drive, whilst overseas batsmen have been more varied in their approach. The vertical, or what is termed the straight bat, is the hallmark of English batsmanship at its best. Yet those great players with the unforgettable names, Hobbs, Sutcliffe, Hammond, Hutton, Washbrook, Compton, May, Cowdrey, Graveney, Barrington, Dexter and more recently, Boycott, were all masters of the back defence in addition to the drive. Currently we see this point confirmed by great batsmen like Greg Chappell of Australia, Viv Richards of the West Indies, Zaheer Abbas of Pakistan, and our own David Gower. Yes, there is not a batsman alive who would not improve his game a lot if he improved his back foot play by a little. Recognise that a straight bat can be presented to the ball horizontally as well as vertically and also take note that those who play strokes off the back foot have much more of the field to aim at than those who play strokes off the front foot. These points are made to give food for thought, for when all is said and done, the truly elegant stroke in cricket is the cover drive played by a master. Perhaps the biggest "getting out" stroke in cricket is the on-drive. Very few batsmen can play it well and we have even discouraged players from trying to play the stroke. Generally they play it badly, and the fault seems to stay with them forever. This may be the stroke that limits your success.

Batsmen are well advised to discuss aspects of batsmanship between themselves and also with their coaches, Sometimes a reduced range of strokes will give a batsman the encouragement to play more to his strengths. By concentrating on playing fewer strokes, not only does he learn to play them better, but almost certainly his confidence will increase and his whole attitude will become more positive. We have seen it happen more than once and we have also heard it said somewhere that the one place batsmen cannot get runs is in the dressing-room! In adopting a positive attitude, a player's role in the team seems to become more effective, especially on the occasions when wickets have to be sacrificed in the quest for quick runs.

Different batsmen naturally have different ways of coping with the first ball they receive and, of course, this in itself depends upon position in the batting order and the state of the game at the time. Many leading batsmen we know take a shorter grip on the bat (drop their bottom hand) when they first go to the wicket. Others concentrate on really watching the ball and not committing themselves to a too early movement of the head. Probably the best tip we can give any batsman when waiting to receive any ball is instead of thinking "how can I stop this ball hitting my wicket?", make a positive effort to say to yourself "how can I score off this ball?". You will be surprised at yourself once you have caught the habit.

There is no doubt about the fact that the "thinking" cricketer is the one to watch and can very often gain a place in the team in front of the more gifted player who may be a "non-thinker".' For example, non-thinking batsmen will play the most magnificent strokes always in the same direction and with the same strength. Similarly, they will defend without the thought of stealing a run. Good opposing captains quickly realise the situation and brief their fielders accordingly. The result is that in frustration the batsman in question gets himself out, trying to play a shot he is not capable of playing. A thinking batsman will always assess the position and ability of the opposing fielders, placing his strokes accordingly.

This also helps in the always difficult art of running between wickets. Everyone on the field should know that on slow pitches the ball tends to go square rather than fine off the bat. On very slow pitches firm-footed driving can be a waste of time and wickets. Without being too committed, batsmen should discuss with their captain what might be a good score under the conditions and in the time available. There are occasions when even the most orthodox batsmen must throw caution to the wind and take calculated risks to hit the ball into vacant parts of the field, or even out of it! A team's innings cannot be planned totally beforehand, but if every batsman plays his part unselfishly, tactics can be planned as the innings progresses. It has been said that bowlers win matches.

As we move on to study the details of the many skills in batting, it is worth repeating that batsmen get themselves out as much by playing the right shot to the wrong ball as playing the wrong shot to the right ball. Think about it! Whichever, there is no doubt that all the practice in the world is no good unless having perfected a stroke, you position yourself to give an identity to the delivery of the ball, whether it be a good length or a half volley or long hop etc. To exaggerate, it is no use trying to play the perfect square-cut to an inswinging half volley!

The basics of batting

To simplify descriptions, it is assumed, unless otherwise stated, that a right-handed batsman is at the wicket. When a batsman is out of form and cannot get a run, even in the best of conditions it is unlikely that the critics will focus their attention on the three factors in batsmanship that may well be the cause of the trouble. That is, the Grip, the Stance, or the Backlift. Yet if a batsman scores a lot of runs, but slowly, the pundits can be expected to put the entire blame on his "peculiar" grip, not his unwillingness to force the pace. A batsman not making runs for two or three innings, obviously because of a bad pitch, may easily find the stance from which he made hundreds only weeks before the subject of a heated debate. Credit or criticism does not always go where it is due, with the result that very often the fundamentals of good batsmanship are ignored until it is too late. We cannot over-emphasise the importance of continuously checking these three foundations of sound technique.

Grip

1. Both hands should be close together, the top hand particularly gripping the handle very firmly. In

normal circumstances approximately one inch of bat handle will protrude.

2. The "vees" formed by thumbs and first fingers should be in line and pointing somewhere between the splice and the outside edge of the bat. The alignment of the "vees" is of the utmost importance. A driver of the ball with a full follow-through will be setting his "vees" as near to the outside edge as his wrist will comfortably allow when playing fully forward defensively. A "check" driver and the defensively inclined batsman will be setting his "vees" more in line with the splice. A compromise is recommended and this should give a batsman the best of both worlds. The important thing is to know what your method is and check it regularly.

Stance

No matter what a batsman's aspirations; no matter what his style, without the sound base of a good stance, his performance is very likely to be limited.

1. The feet are positioned on either side of the batting crease approximately a bat's width apart. Too narrow a stance loses balance, too wide a stance reduces mobility. Weight should be evenly distributed on both feet, never entirely on the heels. The back foot should be parallel to the crease, the front foot either parallel or slightly open (pointing to cover point).

2. The knees are slightly flexed to encourage quick movement of the feet when necessary. Hips are slightly more open than the shoulders.

3. The back of the top hand will generally face between mid-off and cover, depending upon the

batsman's preference for angling the bat in his stance. The side of the top hand rests very lightly against the thigh.

4. Line the shoulders up to point straight down the pitch when a right-arm bowler is bowling over the wicket. If the bowler should change his delivery position, the batsman should change his shoulder line accordingly.

5. The head should be turned fully towards the bowler, with the eyes as level as possible.

6. Do not crouch. Stand as "tall" as possible and always feel comfortable in your stance.

Neither the head nor the feet should move until the ball has been properly sighted and the length judged. Nature being what it is, the ideal positions noted are not always attainable by all batsmen and allowances can be made. For example, those who cannot remain sideways with their eyes level, may open their stance slightly. That is, allow the shoulder to point more towards mid-on. When playing at the ball on or outside the off-stump however, a pronounced shoulder turn will be needed to achieve the correct position to strike the ball. Others, rather than open their stance, will lift their bat off the ground in the stance position to retain the classic body position.

Batsmen who have succeeded with this open stance are Ken Barrington of England and one of the most prolific run scorers of all time, the great Bill Ponsford of Australia. More recently, Peter Willey of Northamptonshire and England has scored centuries against West Indian fast bowling from an open stance, and again from the photographs of the distant past, George Gunn, Maurice Leyland and even Sir Jack Hobbs were not exactly orthodox. The bat lifters, include Dr. W. G. Grace himself and in recent years, Tony Greig. In fact, the really tall batsmen seem to have no choice, if they are not to crouch. Of current players, Graham Gooch is the best example of a bat lifter.

When a batsman goes to the wicket, prior to him receiving the first ball, he asks the umpire to give him a guard. That is, by holding the bat vertically in front of the wicket, the toe of the bat resting on the crease, he is able to mark (scratch) the batting crease in such a way that he knows exactly where he stands in relation to the wicket when in the stance position.

Backlift

Without a well-grooved and technically sound backlift, no batsman can hope to achieve any consistency in striking the ball.

1. Start the backlift early before any other movement, so that the actual stroke is not rushed.

2. Let the top hand take control.

3. Extend the front arm backwards to give a wide sweep with a minimum flex of the elbow.

4. Let the wrists cock naturally to open the bat face.

5. Allow the front forearm to be at least parallel to the ground with the wrist finishing higher than the elbow.

6. Let the shoulder be "pulled" under the chin, the eyes closely watching the bowler's hand.

7. Try to pick the bat up in a line between wicket and wicket. Some very successful batsmen, including Sir Donald Bradman, have picked the bat up towards first and even second slip, but photographs tell us that they "loop" at the top to give a straight downswing towards the ball and through the intended line of stroke.
8. Allow the elbows to clear the body for the high backlift.
9. Keep the head still.

Back strokes

In all back strokes the back foot should remain parallel to the crease throughout its initial movement.

Batsmen should learn to play the attacking strokes before they learn to defend. The theory is that if they learn to defend first, they will become restricted and never ever be able to hit the ball hard. One thing is certain; if a batsman does not have a sound defence, he will not remain at the wicket long enough to play many attacking strokes.

Defensive back stroke

Played to:

1. A short of a length delivery pitched on the wickets, or just outside the off-stump
2. A good length delivery pitched on the wickets or just outside the off-stump, depending upon the technique of the batsman concerned and the prevailing conditions.

It is fair to say that in defence, batsmen tend to play back to the faster bowlers and forward to the slower bowlers.

Batsmen are dismissed far more often when trying to play this stroke than the forward defensive. This results in a general encouragement to play forward, rather than learning to play back correctly. Hence the saying "if in doubt, push out". Whilst the back defensive stroke is the more difficult stroke to learn, it is worth persevering with for the dividends it will pay later.

Checkpoints

1. From a sound stance and backlift, the front shoulder moves just inside the line of the ball, the head leading the balance of the body forward,
2. At the same time, the back foot is taken back parallel with the crease and as far as possible, commensurate with the speed of the ball.
3. The weight is almost entirely on the ball of the back foot, the knee being slightly flexed. The front foot acts only as a balance.
4. The top hand infirm control brings the bat face down the line of the ball, with the front elbow high and bent to an approximate right angle.
5. A light thumb and forefinger grip by the bottom hand, with the elbow tucked in to the side, keeps the bat vertical.
6. There is no follow-through, the bat handle being angled forward to keep the ball down.
7. Throughout the stroke, the head remains down behind the ball, the eyes looking over or round the bat handle.

Attacking back strokes

Forcing shot

Played to:

1. A short of a length delivery pitching just outside the line of wicket.
2. A long hop that keeps low, or a low full toss.

This stroke is becoming one of the most important in the game for a number of reasons:

1. Along with the drive it covers the widest scoring area, ranging from cover to wide mid-on.
2. When played with a "check finish", it is the safest of all the attacking strokes, becoming increasingly popular amongst top-class batsmen as a "bread and butter" stroke that can be played with control off the nagging short of a length delivery.
3. When played with a full follow-through, it is again the safest of the really hard hit strokes.

Checkpoints

1. Follow the basic movements of the back defensive stroke, but with different intention.
2. Make maximum use of your height. Standing with your weight mainly on the ball of your back foot, hit from a firm base.
3. Hitting the ball hard, the rear shoulder drives under the chin, taking the hands high in the full follow-through, as shown in the photograph.

The check finish

This technique requires the wrists to remain firm at impact, rather than breaking them to give a full follow-through. The top elbow remains bent to an approximate right angle throughout the stroke, giving support to the check action, which continues until the stroke is complete.

Whilst the check finish enables some young players to force the ball more easily and correctly on both sides of the wicket, it is important for them also to learn to play the forcing shot with the full follow-through. This applies particularly when given the opportunity to hit a rank bad ball. Obviously with a full follow-through the ball can be hit much harder, if not with quite the same control.

Pull stroke

Played to:

1. A long hop (missing the wicket).
2. A short delivery pitched outside the leg-stump that bounces normally, but never more than chest height.

Move quickly into position and take extra care to watch the ball onto the bat.

Checkpoints

1. Begin this stroke with the basic backlift and movements for the back defensive
2. As the back foot pivots, the body opens and the ball is hit at full arm stretch as the weight transfers to the other foot (left for right-handed batsmen).
3. When pulling the short delivery of such a pace that complete weight transfer is not possible, take care not to fall away from the ball too early. This can easily produce a half-hit stroke off the top edge of the bat.

4. The balance should be forward towards the pitch of the ball as much as possible throughout this stroke.

5. Take care to direct the stroke in front of square-leg by getting the head right behind the line of the ball, and hit the ball down.

The hook stroke

Played to a fast, very short, rising delivery pitched on the stumps or just outside the leg-stump, reaching the batsman above chest height.

This stroke should only be attempted by experienced and very capable batsmen. If played well, it has a high tactical value, but even so should only be used with discretion. Be prepared to "duck" if you are not in the right position to play the stroke and above all, do not take your eyes off the ball.

Checkpoints

1. Follow the same mechanics for this stroke as for the pull, taking care in this case to position your head outside (off-side) the line of the ball, so that if missed, it will go over the left shoulder (right-handed batsman).

2. Quick footwork will enable you to direct the ball square or fine. Concentrate on this aspect of the stroke. It is possible to hook a ball higher, but trying to hit the high ball down is not recommended. In most instances, it is simply not possible.

Comment

An essential stroke for the free-scoring batsman and a prolific run-getter for its best exponents. Take care not to "make room" for this stroke by backing away from the line of the ball.

Checkpoints

1. From a sound stance and backlift, the front shoulder and head turn just inside the line of the ball.
2. The weight is taken completely on the back foot, which automatically moves across and points approximately in the direction of the intended stroke (ideally between point and cover point).
3. A flexible back knee allows the bat to be presented to the ball in as horizontal a plane as possible.
4. From a high backlift, the ball is hit easily at full arm stretch. The bottom hand controls the stroke and the wrists roll enough to direct the ball and keep it down.
5. The back shoulder drives under the chin, allowing a long follow-through of the arms.

The late-cut

Played to:

1. A short of a length delivery wide of the off-stump.
2. This stroke is played to a ball that is not so wide as that to which the square-cut is played.

An elegant old-fashioned stroke now coming back into its own, as limited-over cricket results in vacant slip positions. A stroke to play when your eye is in; not before.

Checkpoints

Similar to the square-cut, but hit closer to the body and

not at full arm stretch. The stroke is played with the wrists and a late hit down, wide of the slips.

The leg-glance (Back Foot)

Played to:

1. A short of a length delivery either pitching leg-stump or just outside, but going down the leg-side.
2. A good length delivery pitching leg-stump or just outside, going down the leg-side.

Take care rot to play this stroke outside the body - it may result in a catch to the wicket-keeper. Neither should the stroke be played to a ball that would hit the wicket.

Checkpoints

Almost up 70 the point of contact play this stroke exactly as the back defensive stroke on the leg-stump. Keep the bat handle forward to keep the ball down, bringing the bottom hand into the stroke as late as possible. Using the wrists, angle the bat and place the ball between square and fine-leg, taking care not to try to hit the ball too fine. This stroke is most effective on fast pitches.

If a vote was taken amongst batsmen, it is sure the front foot drives would come out on top as being the most exhilarating strokes in cricket. At the same time, the mishit drive is perhaps the stroke that gives the bowler his best return, whether the catch be at deep mid-off or in the slips. It is important therefore, to recognise the good length delivery that necessitates a more circumspect forward defensive stroke, which, whilst it is the easier of the two defensive strokes to play, still needs the background of a sound technique.

Forward defensive strokes

The most commonly used stroke in English cricket, probably developed to the state it is because of the old adage "if in doubt, push out". If not, it is certainly a product of the "not getting out" philosophy. Of course, this is an essential and primary stroke in the repertoire of any batsman.

Played to:

A good length ball pitching on the wickets or just outside the off-stump.

The main problem in playing the forward defensive stroke is making the forward movement of the front foot too early, before picking up the line and judging the length of the ball.

Checkpoints

1. From a sound stance and backlift, lead with the front shoulder and head just inside the line of the ball.
2. The hips will follow the shoulder, as will the front leg and foot.
3. The front foot moves as far as comfortably possible towards and just inside the line of the ball.
4. The front knee bends just beyond the vertical, keeping the bail down if it is edged on to the front pad. It also closes the gap between bat and pad.
5. The weight is almost entirely on the front foot. The back leg is fully extended and grounded on the inside of the foot
6. There is no follow-through, as the bat handle is angled forward by a very firm top hand grip and a light thumb and forefinger bottom hand grip.

7. The front elbow is high and at an approximate right angle, keeping the bat face vertical and on the line of the ball.

8. The head is well forward and down towards the pitch of the ball.

Attacking forward strokes

The drives

The check drive: The name "check drive" has only recently been coined, although the stroke itself has been played, albeit sparingly, since cricket was first played. Almost certainly it was firs played accidentally through batsmen using too heavy a bat. Bearing in mind that many young batsmen still use too heavy a bat, it is not illogical for us to analyse the stroke. In fact, experiment has shown that many batsmen find the check drive much easier to play than the full follow-through drive. It introduces a greater element of control, if not of satisfaction. It is, in fact, not very different in execution to the normal full follow-through drive, except in its finish. This is limited through a locked or checked wrist and a very high right-angled elbow joint, just as described for the check finish of the forcing back stroke. You should have the feeling that the power is going into the stroke through the back of the elbow. If you can play the drive with a full follow-through, do so—you will find it much more exciting. At the same time, learning the check drive will give you the advantage of a "second string".

The off-drive

Played to:

A half volley pitched on or just outside the off-stump.

Technically, the off-drive follows all the initial movements of the forward defensive stroke, but with a very different intention in the final execution of the stroke. Recognising the opportunity of making contact with the ball on the half volley, the batsman is looking to accelerate the bat through the ball along the line of the intended stroke.

Checkpoints

1. The front shoulder leads the front foot just inside the line of the ball.
2. The full face of the bat comes down the line of the stroke.
3. The eyes watch the bat hit the ball on the half volley.
4. The rear shoulder drives under the chin, giving a full extension of the bottom arm through the line of the stroke.
5. Wrists will lock for the check drive and break for the full follow-through, the hands finishing high.

The cover drive

Played as for the off-drive with a more pronounced shoulder turn into the line of the wider ball, which should be what you will recognise as a wide half volley. Avoid playing the cover drive early in your Innings to the swinging or turning ball, especially on a doubtful pitch.

The on-drive

Played to:

A half volley pitched on or just outside the let-stump.

We have already spoken of the difficulty in playing this stroke. As in all driving, the shoulder and head should lead the stroke, but it is in the on-drive that the head seems to so easily fall over towards the off-side, causing the body to overbalance and throw the bat off the line of the stroke. A good tip is to drop the front shoulder slightly leading into the stroke.

1. As in all strokes, but particularly this one, stand tall, keeping your head well over your base.
2. Avoid hitting too hard.
3. Make sure you are well over the ball.
4. Along with the cover drive, do not try to drive the ball too square.

Lofted drives, whether they are off, on, or straight, should only be intended to be hit over the in-fielders into the open spaces of the field or even for six. Most batsmen would be virtually giving their wickets away trying to hit the ball over the boundary fielder.

Checkpoints

1. Follow all the points for the full drives, finishing with hands high. No half measures!
2. Avoid leaning back. Hit the ball just short of the half volley.

Moving out to drive

There is one common factor that shows itself clearly in all good batsmen—correct and quick footwork. Being in the right position to execute a stroke is an essential part of batsmanship. If you are not in the right position, you cannot play the stroke, it is as simple as that. Once a bowler knows that he is bowling to a batsman who can use his feet, his tactics are limited and the batsman can more easily dominate. Moving down the pitch is a ploy that only needs to be used when the bowler has the initiative. The secret is in keeping a good balance and retaining the poise that is given by leading with the shoulder and head from a good stance.

Checkpoints

1. Following the first stride of the front foot, the back foot moves just behind it, staying parallel to the crease to maintain the original sideways position.
2. The front foot is again lead by the front shoulder, as in the normal drive.

As an example, through the early sighting of a flighted ball, a good length can be turned into a half volley and consequently punished. If you do use this tactic of moving down the pitch, be realistic. If you have misjudged the length and there is the chance of you being left "high and dry", play defensively - do not go through with the stroke. Be sure to keep "in front" of the ball and do not throw your innings away, giving the wicket-keeper an easy stumping.

Leg-glance (Front Foot)

Played to.

A good length ball (slightly over-pitched) pitching on or just outside the leg-stump, but going down the leg-side

Take care not to play this stroke outside the body —it may result in a catch to the wicket-keeper. Neither should the stroke be played to a ball that would hit the wicket

Checkpoints

Commence the stroke as if you were playing forward defensive stroke, but position your front pad to meet the ball if it is missed by the bat. Keeping the bat vertical, turn the wrists just before contact, keep the handle to forward and aiming square on the leg-side, rather than fine. The hands "flick" through a well-controlled stroke.

The sweep

Played to:

A good length ball pitched outside the leg-stump and turning in towards the wicket. The stroke can also be played as an alternative to the front foot leg-glance, i.e. to a ball pitching on or outside the leg-stump and going down the leg-side.

A modern stroke developed to combat the good length ball on slow turning pitches Also it can be an alternative to moving down the pitch to drive, even on good pitches, when the occasion demands.

Checkpoints

1. Commence the stroke as though playing the forward defensive.
2. From a high backlift, make contact with the ball just after it pitches, i.e. on the half volley.
3. Hit the ball down and direct it behind square-leg or finer, if necessary.
4. Let the front leg bend fully, allowing the back leg to trail.
5. The ball should hit the front pad if the bat fails to make contact.

General qualifications

Some people are born with this natural aptitude--this ball sense--this physical co-ordination; others can never achieve it. The greatest of players can improve by means of concentration and practice but the natural athlete must start with a great advantage. One hall-mark of good batting is that the player appears to have plenty of time in which to play his shots. In theory one could make out a case for standing still and not moving the bat until you see the ball in the air and know where it is pitching.

In practice this doesn't happen, and I am all in favour of the batsman starting to lift his bat and making a preliminary movement with his feet before the ball is actually delivered.

It saves a precious fraction of a second and appears to serve the same purpose as the preliminary waggle before starting your swing at golf. It is not part of the swing but it gets you started.

Physique does not seem to follow any predetermined pattern. The Test match records are shared by men of all shapes and sizes, from the rotund Warwick Armstrong to the diminutive Lindsay Hassett, the tall and graceful Frank Woolley to the short, rather hunched Clarrie Grimmett and the gloriously athletic Walter Hammond. Then who shall define temperament? The dictionary gives the word a meaning though from a cricket sense I find it unsatisfactory.

More important still, nobody can tell you how to acquire a good temperament if it is lacking in your basic nature.

Some players are marvellous at the nets but cannot reproduce their form in matches. Others are poor net players but succeed because they possess the so-called "big match temperament." A tremendous premium must be placed on this peculiar characteristic, which is probably more essential for a batsman than any form of sport I can think of.

The golfer may fluff his drive, the tennis player miss his smash and so on, there is still time to recover, but one mistake by a batsman and there is no second chance. Hand in hand with temperament must go concentration, which can and must be cultivated by anyone who wishes to rise to international standards. It is one of the essentials.

Moreover, the concentration needs to be harnessed for long periods. Many batsmen can survive a short period, say half an hour' and score double figures, but they are unable to keep going. Test cricket demands the utmost concentration for hours on end.

The two most important pieces of advice I pass on to young batsmen are to (a) concentrate and (b) watch the ball.

They could well be the last words before anyone goes in to bat. Watching the ball means that the batsman must first carefully observe the bowler's hand as he is in the act of delivering the ball. The movement of hand and arm gives the first clue as to the bowler's intentions--whether he is trying to impart off spin, leg spin or something else. Once the ball leaves the hand, the ball must be the sole object of your attention.

Undoubtedly some people have keener eyesight than others. The wizard RanjitsinhJi was supposed to see the ball very clearly. Indeed, there is a story that a certain prominent batsman on being questioned as to his own ability to see the ball said, "Yes, I had good eyesight--I could see the seams, but Ranji could see the stitches." In his early years a batsman should be able to see the ball turning in the air as it comes down the pitch towards him when the bowler is a slow spinner.

This is necessary against a class googly bowler like Arthur Mailey. Even if he disguises his googly you still have the added insurance of watching the spin of the ball to make sure which way it will turn on pitching. Try to glue the eyes on the ball until the very moment it hits the bat. This cannot always be achieved in practice but try.

Blessed is the boy who finds himself possessed of these attributes as a natural gift. But like the boy prodigy who, at, say, five years of age, finds himself able to play the piano, practice and more practice is needed to perfect his talent.

The fellow who sees the ball leave the bowler's hand, sees it land and then plays "at the pitch," is always in trouble when the ball moves in the air or after hitting the ground.

When it comes to detailed execution of the art, batting at the nets is the first method of improving one's efficiency. So many things can be tried out there.

You can experiment with your grip, your stance, stroke execution, etc., until satisfied you have the right method.

Throughout his career a batsman, even though he may have achieved fame, must continue assiduously at net practice.

That notable left-handed opening batsman Warren Bardsley once made a century in a Test match and, so we are told, went straight out to the practice nets because he was dissatisfied with his form.

Confidence in one's own ability is admirable in moderation but it does not absolve anyone from the need for practice.

The early formative years of a boy's career can have a tremendous bearing on his technique.

Take full advantage of your natural assets, improve them and adapt them to changing circumstances. It is a good idea to try to obtain net practice against the type of bowler who worries you most, or against whom you expect to play in forthcoming matches.

An outstanding example of this need was the 1956 tour of England by Australia. To the most casual observer it was obvious the Australians were having more trouble with off-spinner Laker than any other type. It was a clear case where net practice against off-spinners was a cardinal need.

Whilst it is true that some players are born, or achieve greatness without coaching, and equally true that some players are overcoached, I still believe in the desirability of sound coaching.

The trouble is that coaches vary just the same as players. They should always build upon and improve existing talent, and seldom is it wise to completely alter anybody's style. One's physical movements are decided by muscular and bodily structure. It would be useless trying to coach the dynamic Learie Constantine to emulate the slow, easy rhythm and grace of Frank

Woolley. But it would be correct for a coach to make sure each man played his drives with the bat reasonably close to the front leg. The value of coaching is to pick out departures from fundamental soundness and build on nature, not to try to mould every player into precisely the same type.

The coach who insists on every batsman having complete control with his top hand is wrong, because it does not suit everyone. I'm sure Denis Compton's genius would never have blossomed if he had been compelled, as a youth, to allow his top hand to become the master.

Conversely Sir Leonard Hutton was a marvellous example of top-hand control. It suited him. The coach must have sufficient intelligence not to be dogmatic but to discern what method is best for his pupil.

For any player the top hand is of supreme importance when playing a forward defensive shot. But when it comes to a full-blooded pull, the story is very different. There cannot be sufficient power without the bottom hand, nor adequate control without the other. Coordination is the thing.

Get into the correct position for your shots and it is marvellous how much easier they become.

Footwork should, generally speaking, be constantly taking the batsman towards the off. Young batsmen have a natural tendency to draw away from a ball directed at the body. This impulse must be overcome.

Don't let that rear foot retreat to the leg side. Almost invariably one should move towards the off, whether it is forward with your left foot or back with your right. By going back with your right foot mean back and towards the stumps--not back towards the umpire.

History shows that the outstanding batsmen were mostly strong off the back foot. They could drive, of course, but their initial protective movement was back rather than forward.

Ranji expressed himself very much in favour of back play, and went on to say, "No forward stroke is absolutely safe unless the ball is smothered." By that I assume he meant it had to be played as a genuine half-volley.

No batsman can fail to get into difficulties if he persists in driving well away from his body, in driving against a turning leg-break and so on.

To some extent footwork is based on judgment, and straight away we revert to the need for practice to acquire judgment. You see how inextricably all these things are interwoven.

Eventually a batsman should reach the stage where his judgment of whether to play forward or back becomes instinctive rather than deliberate. The sight of the ball seems to trigger off a corresponding reaction so that movement becomes almost a habit.

All bowlers deteriorate under a well-planned, intelligent attack and much of the enjoyment of batting comes from the battle of wits and the thwarting of a bowler's plans.

Any batsman who has achieved international status should be able to visualise the position of every fieldsman just as though he were looking at them on a radar screen. He should be able to shut his eyes and know precisely the location of fine-leg, third-man and so on. In no other way can he concentrate on the ball and still give free reign to the art of placing the ball to the maximum advantage.

It is so simple to pull a short ball to square-leg. But if there is a man on the fence square, how much more satisfaction can be gained by deliberately pulling it finer to try and pick up four.

There are dozens of shots played in any long innings which can scarcely be described as drives, pulls, cuts, or by any authentic name. They may range from a deflection down the gully with a perpendicular bat to a pat towards cover for a single or a push towards mid-on.

Batting is a fascinating art and worth all the study you can give it.

The grip

Having dealt with certain generalities, I now turn to the important details of the actual playing side of cricket.

A splendid coach was asked by a lad what was the correct grip. The coach told the boy to lay his bat face down on the ground with the handle pointing towards him and then to stoop down and pick it up with two hands as though proposing to use it.

The boy did and was immediately told that was his proper grip.

Try it out and see what result you get. Notice that the inverted V formed by the thumb and first finger of the right hand is straight in line with the insertion of the handle down the back of the blade. The bottom hand will be an inch or two from the shoulder of the blade. This is what might be termed, in golfing parlance, a slightly shut face. I think it helps to keep the ball on the ground, especially when playing on-side strokes.

The Hobbs grip is very common amongst Englishmen, whereas one would seldom find a player with his left wrist more behind the blade than mine. The two hands should be very close to one another--in fact just about touching when the batting gloves are on.

One fine Sheffield Shield cricketer had his right hand so far down the handle that his index finger actually went along the back of the blade. As you might expect, he had good defensive control and played strokes behind the wicket splendidly but his driving was incompetent.

There is much to be said in favour of keeping the two hands in the happy medium position for maximum power and control.

The left-hand position must remain firm irrespective of the attempted stroke, but the right, hand may be allowed to move down the blade for greater control in defensive strokes.

As evidence of the difference of the left-hand position of great players in playing defensively, I cannot do better than refer you to the photographs of May and Compton.

Peter May's method suited me, but Denis Compton's wonderful record dares us to question the efficiency of his.

As further evidence that leading players very often follow the habit of dropping the right hand down the blade when playing defensively, look at the photograph of thc Grand Old Man, W. G. Grace.

Sometimes we dropped the hand down when square cutting or in pulling the ball, but the movement must be so natural that the player is scarcely conscious of it, for one has little time to think where his hands are when moving into a shot. Whatever you do be comfortable and natural and make control your guiding star.

The stance

Once again we refuse to lay down any hard and fast unalterable rules, because Test players have been successful with quite different stances. However, there are certain principles which can be enunciated. The main purpose of this initial position when awaiting delivery of the ball is to be in such a comfortably relaxed and well-balanced position that you are able to go forward or back, attack or defend, with equal speed.

The knees should be slightly relaxed. It is a mistake to crouch right over or to stand completely erect. Notice that the feet are about six inches apart and that the weight is equally distributed.

The rear foot should be at least a couple of inches behind the batting crease. This is to allow for a slight drag when playing forward. Remember the foot must be behind the crease to avoid a stumping. On the line is out. The front foot should be parallel to the batting crease and some three inches in front of it. Should the front toe be turned slightly towards cover that would not be wrong. Looking down the pitch from the bowler's end, the batsman's toes should be just about in line with the leg stump.

This position encourages a straighter back lift, is perhaps sounder for defensive play. It will be seen from the photographs that the batting gloves rest lightly against the left pad. There is a possibility that the batting glove may get caught in the top of the pad.

As mentioned earlier this might be likened to what is termed a preliminary "waggle" in golf.

Cricket, too, possesses its "waggles" or mannerisms.

W. G. Grace had a similar mannerism. In fact Sir Jack may have copied him. Old Phil Mead touched his cap to the square-leg umpire then patted the ground four times and took four tiny shuffling steps to his position before every ball. It was just part of his method of becoming relaxed and comfortable.

The left shoulder should be pointing down the pitch or very nearly so, with the head turned so that both eyes are clearly focused on the bowler. One often hears about the two-eyed stance. This is a misnomer. What people really mean is a stance where the shoulders are turned so that the chest is facing the bowler. A chesty stance is wrong because it prevents the batsman getting into the correct driving position. But obviously nobody would be silly enough to try to watch the bowler with one eye only.

That may sound absurd, for obviously the head must move if the body does. But we mean to convey the impression that there should be no bobbing or weaving about and that any jerky movement which might cause a batsman to take his eye off the flight of the ball is dangerous.

Perhaps we should exclude the case where one has to duck quickly to avoid a bumper, but I'll deal with that later. Concentrate the eyes on the ball and it is surprising how natural the body movement becomes. Once again comfort and relaxation are the key words.

Taking guard or block

Every batsman, upon arriving at the crease, must take block. There are three common positions; middle stump, leg stump, and two legs (meaning halfway between the middle stump and the leg stump).

The sole purpose of taking guard is to enable the batsman to judge the direction of the ball relative to his wicket. The striker will, upon getting the required position, mark it on the ground back from the popping crease.

Spectators sometimes wonder why batsmen may ask for guard several times during an innings. The answer is that a mark on the ground may become obliterated or damaged. Occasionally the two batsmen at the wickets take a different block or one may be a left-hander. Obviously the one is inclined to make rather a mess of the other fellow's mark, especially if he is the nervous type who is constantly patting the ground whilst awaiting delivery of the ball. The sprigs can also tear across one's mark when making certain foot movements.

When an off-break bowler is operating to a strong leg field, many batsmen take guard on the leg stump or even, in extreme cases, just outside. By so doing they endeavour to counter his wiles. They feel it gives them greater freedom to hit at any ball directed at their pads, and a better chance of steering away from the clutching hands of leg slips any ball directed at the stumps. There is much to be said for the theory.

On the other hand a batsman whose great weakness is that he fails to cover the ball outside the off-stump, especially against a fast or medium-pace attack, would be wise to consider taking middle stump for his guard. It would take him those extra couple of inches towards the line of flight before the ball is delivered. So take your choice. You will have to stand or fall by your judgment.

The back lift

Reams of matter have been written about the necessity of taking one's bat back perfectly straight. Some coaching books even advocate taking the bat back over the stumps.

Too many players fail because their thoughts are concentrated on where their left elbow is or where something else is, instead of hitting the ball.

For defensive shots the bat should naturally be as straight as possible, but for a pull shot, for instance, a perfectly straight back lift would make it far harder to execute the stroke.

In a sensible back lift and agree that it should not be that of the muscular man who strikes the gong in the J. Arthur Rank films, but there must be some degree of latitude and it must not become an obsession clogging up stroke production. By going to extremes the player who uses the crease area and takes the bat back absolutely straight would find himself out hit wicket. So long as the batsman is in the correct position at the top of the back lift, we don't think he can go far wrong.

If we could take moving pictures of all leading batsmen in action, particularly when they were not conscious that a camera was focused on them, we think we would find the majority of them take the blade back rather, more towards first or second slip. That initial movement probably allows a flexibility which the strictly orthodox does not.

Even that arch disciple of a straight bat, Trevor Bailey, offends the text book as much as we do in making some strokes. The strip photographs in his book illustrating various shots clearly show the back lift is not always straight. His bat, like mine, is sometimes taken back towards the slip fieldsmen, but of course it comes down straight.

And even W. G. Grace, with his famous "left-wrist in front of the handle" grip lifted his bat up towards slips, as you will see from the precious photograph below. We say precious because the movie film from which this photograph was reproduced was taken over fifty years ago and is believed to be the only film ever made of W.G.

Whether the bat is taken back straight towards the stumps or towards first slip, be careful it is not too high. Remember that the higher the back lift the longer it will take to bring the bat down. There is always a happy medium, but the back lift should be no higher than is necessary for a proper balance between control in defence and power in attack.

Everything in batting leads up to stroke play which may be divided into (a) defensive shots and (b) attacking shots.

Again each may be classified into two sections, (a) strokes played with the weight predominantly on the front foot, (b) strokes played with the weight predominantly on the back foot.

Footwork

How often have we heard the saying "Jones is a great batsman--his footwork is superb." What is meant by this term footwork ?

It is not a question which can be answered simply, even though instinctively a cricketer knows what is meant.

Most people would say good footwork implies correct footwork. Perhaps it does. But what is the use of a man going back on to his stumps in the approved fashion if he moves so slowly that he is late in completing his shot and is trapped LBW. This surely means one requires speed as well. But too much speed may bring disaster. If one jumps out to drive, gets there too soon and lofts a catch, that could be fatal.

These reflections cause to say that basically, to be good, footwork should be correct, it should be of the required speed and it must be coordinated with perfect judgment. Certainly it should never be too slow.

One of the outstanding characteristics of great players is the apparent ease with which they play their shots. They always seem to be in the right position with plenty of time to spare.

Back defence

When playing back defensively, the back lift should be as straight as conveniently possible, and that in its downward path the bat should pass just outside the right pad as it comes forward to meet the ball.

Suppose you are playing back to an off-break pitched a couple of inches outside the off stump, and the ball, after pitching, turns across on to the middle and leg stumps. It would no longer be any use playing dead straight towards the pitch of the ball. It would be necessary to follow the direction of the ball, and to do this some power or impetus must come from the right hand which can't therefore be entirely relaxed. That change of direction to follow the ball cannot satisfactorily be controlled by the left hand.

Also it is possible to move into position for a back defensive stroke but later convert it into an attacking shot if you see fit to do so.

But when purely on the defensive there should be little or no follow through. At least the left hand must be powerful enough to restrict any tendency to follow through too soon, whereby off a rising ball there might be a catch to a close-in fieldsman.

Coinciding with the initial movement of taking the bat back, the right foot must be moved back and across in front of the stumps. The left foot is automatically brought across so that the stumps are completely protected.

In case you think the position of the left leg is unimportant, just have a glance at the photograph below of Freddie Brown being bowled. The bail has obviously come back from the off side and, without a protective left leg, has got through. Incidentally, Freddie's expression is lovely. What do you think he is saying? Advantage should be taken of the area between the batting crease and the stumps, a distance of four feet. Obviously one cannot go back the full distance, but even two feet extra in which to sight the ball helps a lot.

Far too many cricketers play back on the popping crease. In other words they go back but not across, making the shot harder in every way.

Some coaches advocate that the toes shall remain parallel with the popping crease--others that they should point towards the bowler.

To be correct the full weight should be taken on the right foot, leaving the movement of the left as more of a balancing medium.

The right hand slides down to the bottom of the handle to give added control though, as I said earlier, the grip is firm.

Study the movie strips and the coordinated movement is easily followed.

Keep the head well over the line of flight and down. Lifting the head is fatal and generally results in cocking the ball up or hitting it on the edge.

It is not a bad idea to practise back and forward defence in front of a mirror to see precisely where your feet are placed and to follow the movement of your bat. So often the player thinks his bat is in the right place but to the onlooker it is wrong. Archie Jackson and Alan Fairfax were renowned for practising in front of a mirror. We have seen them do it for an hour at a time. Whilst there are limitations in other directions, I certainly favour the idea for practising back and forward defensive shots, because your eyes remain looking straight ahead.

Forward defence

This type of defensive stroke should be used when the ball is pitched farther up than a good length and is on, or very close to, a direct line between the two sets of stumps. Its purpose is to smother any spin or swing which may be on the ball. Supposing the ball was spinning so much that it changed course from leg to off five degrees on hitting the ground. If allowed to travel a mere six inches after pitching before hitting the blade, this deviation would not matter. But if allowed to travel a few feet, it might touch the edge of the bat for a catch in the slips. Obviously, therefore, to play forward to a short-pitched ball is bad theory.

It is desirable in forward play to keep the bat absolutely perpendicular throughout, therefore a reasonably straight back lift is required. The handle of the bat should be kept forward of the blade in order that the ball will be kept down. Always play close to the front leg so that the ball cannot get between bat and pad.

The left shoulder and elbow should lean forward towards the pitch of the ball and really drag the front foot and the body forward. Bend the left knee slightly to hold the weight of the body in balance and point the left toe towards mid-off or cover, varying it slightly according to the direction of the ball.

If the ball is pitched on' the leg stump, for instance, the left toe will point more towards the bowler than it would be for a ball pitched, say, just outside the off stump.

Keep the head well forward and down. At the end of the stroke the right toe will be the balancing agent at the rear (right heel off the ground) and it must be kept firmly behind the batting crease. This precaution is necessary in case the ball misses the bat and the question of a stumping arises.

One of cricket's simplest errors is for a batsman to misjudge the length of a ball, play forward and be beaten by spin or swing. The tendency then is to over. balance forward--hence the need for keeping that right toe firmly down.

In forward defence the left hand is in control.

Note how the right-hand grip has changed until it has become almost a thumb and first two fingers only at the bottom of the handle. The right hand acts really as a guide. No power is required.

Back cut or late cut

Modern players tend to eschew the late cut altogether and their expressed reason is "too dangerous". Providing proper judgment is used the rewards to be gained from the shot are well worth the risk. It should only be attempted when the ball is reasonably short of a length and not bouncing very high but is pitched well outside the off stump--it is cut rather in the direction of third or even second slip--and instead of hitting at right angles to the flight as with a square cut, the bat runs in an extreme case a most parallel with the line of flight at contact. The ball is actually hit down on to the ground. It is normally on the rise when struck and therefore a snick is almost certain to result in a catch to the wicket-keeper. That is why extreme care and precision are required. It is usually unsafe to try the stroke against fast bowlers. The safety margin is too small and, anyway, fast bowlers usually have slip fieldsmen who would be in the way.

Likewise it is very dangerous against off-spinners, but against medium-pace or leg-break bowlers there is a good chance of reward. Power comes mainly from the wrists, but the ball's own momentum is the chief source of its speed. The stroke is a short, snappy one and not a long swing.

After contact with the ball, the end of the bat should go straight down and almost hit the ground. In fact some players do actually hit the ground. This is a good indication of playing the shot correctly. Whether to risk the stroke or not will be governed by the type of pitch and bowler and the position of the fieldsmen. It may not be worth while for a chancy single, but it may well be if a certain four is in the offing.

One contemporary Test batsman of mine played it with only moderate success because he invariably started to transfer his weight to his front foot (as though anxious to start running) as he was hitting the ball. This action militates against watching the ball and very often drags the batsman out of his correct position, so that as often as not he cuts the ball too straight into the ground or gets it on the inside edge, sometimes pulling it on to the stumps.

9

WICKET-KEEPING

Great fieldsmen naturally play an important role in any team. A Gregory or Hammond in the slips, a Jack Hobbs in the covers or a Constantine anywhere can do much to uplift the fielding, but nothing has such an electrical effect upon the fielding morale as a wicket-keeper who brings off seemingly impossible stumpings and dives to hold phenomenal catches. The very nature of the game means that these opportunities come his way so much more often than they do to other fielders.

It was at once a lesson. There is perfect timing in the catching of a cricket ball just the same as there is in batting. Just a You get the sweet sound from a perfectly struck cover drive, so you do from the gloves.

How many thousands of times since 1921 have we heard the same sound, and when trying to judge the class of a young 'keeper, it is one of the first things I look (or listen) for.

Each had very special virtues and it is not my wish here to offer comparisons, except to refer to individual characteristics.

It is notable that the two outstanding qualities of great 'keepers are timing and footwork.

Godfrey Evans displayed more agility than anyone can remember and he also possessed astonishing energy. In fact, his whole effervescent personality, his infectious humour and obvious enjoyment of the task, must have been a great inspiration to many England teams.

This enthusiasm is something every 'keeper could try to emulate, no other fieldsman has anything like the same opportunities of inspiring his colleagues.

What special requirements does this job call for? Very high on the list we would place courage. Few men have stood behind the stumps during a long career without suffering severe physical injury.

In normal work the hands take a fairly heavy pounding. The early pioneers of the field, men like J. M. Blackham, wore gloves more akin to the present-day walking-out gloves. No wonder they initially had long-stops and that their hands finished up resembling gnarled oak. Broken fingers and busted joints were not by any means uncommon.

The wickets in the early days were ill prepared and moreover there was some wild bowling. In the 1843 Oxford v. Cambridge match no less than 82 wides were chalked up. What a sensation that would cause today. It is even recorded that Little Dench of Brighton, fielding at long-stop, had a sack of straw tied to his chest to prevent injury.

The modern heavily padded gloves, with finger-stalls and inner gloves, help to protect the hands from injury, but even today most 'keepers take the precaution of binding their top finger joints with adhesive tape to minimise the damage from a blow on the end of the finger. It was freely stated that George Duckworth put a steak in the palm of his right glove to soften the blows when he was 'keeping to Harold Larwood.

Most wicket-keepers have received blows in the face or on the head to say nothing of plenty on the body. They are unavoidable at times even by the most skilful. Wickets of all kinds, including sticky ones, are encountered. There is the occasional mishap such as a ball flying up off the top of a stump when a batsman is bowled. One such happening badly cut Langley's eye and put him out of a Test match. And apart from the danger of injury, the 'keeper must keep going and maintain his concentration throughout the longest and hottest days without flagging.

His job is not finished when the ball has been delivered, for then he frequently has to run up to the stumps and try to take a nasty, inaccurate return from the field, endeavouring to convert it miraculously into a run-out. To force the hand and nerve and sinew to serve their turn long after they are tired out demands much moral as well as physical courage.

Fitness then is an important and valuable asset to any wicket-keeper.

Practice for wicket-keeping

The people who devise practice wickets seldom think of the Aunt Sally. Have a look next time you see a practice area and you will probably find in most instances that the rear net is so close to the stumps that there would be little room in which a wicket-keeper could operate.

Recently I saw a case where the bats man, playing back, actually caught his bat handle in the overhanging net with a resultant nasty crack in the face

It is a good idea to have at least six or eight feet between the stumps and the rear net so that a 'keeper would have room in which to move.

Perhaps this inattention to practice facilities is one reason why you seldom notice wicket-keepers practising at the nets. They may also be fearful of damaging their hands or receiving an injury of some other kind, for undoubtedly wicket-keeping holds more hazards than other branches of cricket.

But nothing produces efficiency like practice, which is the best way to learn how to avoid those injuries.

I am a believer in sessions between the bowler and the `keeper without a batsman, especially when the bowler is of the slow, tricky type, so that his stumper can get to understand the wrist and finger movement without having to worry about his opponent.

It is fatal if the bowler's own wicket-keeper can't spot his wrong-run.

Equipment

The most important parts of the outfit must be the gloves--inner and outer. As an instrument is to a musician, they are the medium through which the player must display his art.

The inner gloves should be of chamois leather and put on slightly damp. The outers should then fit snugly over the top. It is a mistake to have them sloppy, and unwise to use new gloves first time in a match. Normally they are stiff and require to be worked in by a fair amount of practice so that they become pliable and form a cup into which the ball snugly fits. Then the gloves need to be faced. The rubber surface tends to become shiny and slippery so a preparation is often used to make it slightly tacky. Neatsfoot oil is commonly applied and so is eucalyptus. Mixed preparations are available in sports shops. The purpose is to have the rubber face properly conditioned, but be careful to see you don't overdo it otherwise this stickiness will be transmitted to the ball.

We have heard many a bowler use harsh language about a 'keeper who overprepared his gloves. The black sticky substance is particularly annoying when it gets on a new ball and thence on to the bowler's fingers. And it militates against the ball swinging, too.

Should special pads be worn? Well, I have seen them with special heavily reinforced tops or even side levers down the outsides of the shins but I distrust them. We feel they make for clumsiness whereas speed is of supreme importance. Pads are only the second line of defence anyway--the hands are the things that really count.

An abdominal protector must be worn. Not only does it protect the wearer from injury--it gives him far greater confidence.

Stumpings

Two points sometimes misunderstood are:--

1. That the batsman's toe must be behind the popping crease;

   and

2. That the wicket-keeper must not take the ball in front of the stumps for the purpose of making a stumping.

How often has one heard a spectator complain about a batsman being out stumped because, so he claimed, the strikers foot was on the line. It may have been but he was still out. The marking of the creases is so designed that the distance allowed by the laws from stumps to batting crease is measured to the inside of the line. Therefore, the foot must be kept behind. On the line is not good enough. It is out.

Regarding the second point, the rule reads:

"The wicket-keeper shall remain wholly behind the wicket until a ball delivered by the bowler touches the bat or person of the striker, or passes the wicket, or until the striker attempts a run."

Note particularly that the law does not merely relate to the wicket-keeper's hands. No part of his person is allowed to be in front of the stumps. Admittedly the hands are the most likely part to transgress the law but the young, eager 'keeper must be careful not to infringe this rule in his excitement to gain a victim. It can easily be done with head or foot when the striker goes well down to a slow spinner and misses. And, of course, it is just another of the many things an umpire has to watch.

Where and how to stand

No hard and fast rules can be laid down under the above heading.

When slow or medium-pace bowlers are operating it is customary for the 'keeper to stand up at the stumps but he goes back to the faster types. There is no doubt it is easier to take snicks behind the wicket (especially on the leg side) when standing back to a fastish bowler than when standing up. Likewise stumping opportunities become more rare as the bowler's pace increases.

Normally, therefore, it becomes a matter of judgment as to which position is likely to yield the better results.

Sometimes special considerations intrude. For instance, Alec Bedser always preferred to have his 'keeper at the stumps even when bowling in-swingers at top speed. For personal reasons Bedser gained confidence and felt better able to give of his best, to exploit his technique to the full.

Godfrey Evans was so often his willing confederate in the English team and what a task he had. Many a time he made an incredible save on the leg side--often he took nasty cracks on the wrist or body, but occasionally he brought off an astounding stumping.

As one of the batsmen who was put to the test by Bedser's theory of a wicket-keeper at the stumps, I can vouch for its correctness in his case. He was a better bowler with Evans at the stumps.

No batsman could afford to play forward and overbalance if he missed an inswinger and I would have been happier as a batsman with Evans standing back.

Admittedly Evans did a marvellous job and very few men, if any, could have taken Bedser as he did.

But we have made the point. A wicket-keeper should stand where he thinks he can achieve the best result, coordinating his ideas with those of the bowler and the captain.

He must stand right up or right back. Halfway, or no-man's land as we call it, is useless.

Wicket-keepers usually stand with the left foot round about the line of the off stump and in this position can obtain a clear view of the bowler's delivery outside that stump., However, there must be a degree of flexibility. He may stand a shade wider, for instance, for a right-hand bowler coming round the wicket than for a left-hander coming round and so on. The main thing is to be comfortable, evenly balanced and to easily pick up the flight of the ball.

If standing at the stumps, he should be sufficiently close to remove the bails with a natural sweeping movement which does not demand any stretching.

When a ball is delivered wide of the wicket there is a natural tendency for the stumper to move across and slightly backwards. The latter should be resisted because it would take him away from the wickets and so make a stumping harder and slower. Foot movement should be kept down to a minimum and confined to the essential ones for positioning the body and hands except where one has difficulty in reaching the ball at all.

A fault which is common with the lower-grade keepers is that they fail to move their bodies with the line of flight or even in advance of it.

If a fast bowler sends down a big inswinger which dips outside the leg stump, the 'keeper has to bear in mind both the saving of byes and the possibility of catching the batsman from a snick on the leg side. Therefore, immediately he picks up the flight and realises what the ball is doing, he should move to the leg side so that if possible he will be able to take the ball still coming towards his body. In this way he will be getting into the correct position to take the ball cleanly and he will have a margin on his left side to take the ball if it is deflected by a snick.

Don Tallon was an artist at this. He often went so fast and so far that he still took the ball on his right-hand side But he took many snicks on his left-hand side which other players would never have reached.

The same principle holds good for out-swingers, namely to move across and still take the ball coming at the body if you can. But, of course, this is an easier proposition as the ball is visible all the way. There is no blind spot with the batsman's body obscuring the vision as there must be with an inswinger outside the legs.

And don't forget to let those hands "give" with the ball, especially off fast bowlers.

Always take the ball, if possible, with the fingers pointing towards the ground and see the hands give slightly as they take the ball. This is to minimise the risk of injury.

Most damaged joints and many broken fingers are caused by accidental blows on the ends of the fingers.

There are times when the fingers cannot be held down, the most difficult of all being the delivery which comes straight at the chest, but at least unnecessary injuries should be avoided.

Long experience and even instinct will prepare a 'keeper for the type of delivery which might produce a stumping chance notably the unbalanced forward stroke. In those crucial moments when split-second judgment is called for, there must be lightning speed and precision. Above all, certainty of taking the ball. Don't snatch at it in your excitement.

It is absolutely vital for the wicket-keeper to watch the ball right into his gloves. He should get his body in front of the line of flight when taking the ball, except when deliberately staying inside for a stumping chance or to avoid being hit.

No player on the field can be so helpful to his bowler and his captain as the 'keeper. He is the man who sees exactly what every ball does. Whether it swings in the air or turns off the pitch--the slightest thing must be noticed. The man at square-leg may see the striker play at but miss a ball near the off stump and form the opinion that it swung away to the off. He may be quite wrong. The ball may have gone straight through, the batsman just simply playing inside it. But the wicket-keeper won't be fooled.

Similarly he can instinctively tell which type of delivery is causing the batsman most concern and can quietly pass on useful tips to the bowlers between overs.

Then, of course, a vital part of the job is to take returns from the field and assist in run-outs. With wild and inaccurate throws the task becomes far more onerous and dangerous than it need be. Many a blow has resulted from a fast throw which landed on the roughened footmarks near the stumps.

Should there be any chance of a run-out, the 'keeper should make position behind the stumps as early as possible and never take the ball in front of them. It is the fieldsmen's job to throw correctly and the 'keeper should do everything possible to encourage and persuade them not to make him an Aunt Sally.

Because of the gloves, he is able to catch a ball with more certainty than anyone else. For this reason, whether it be a snick on the off or leg, or even a skied mishit.

In the modern era we sometimes feel the emphasis *has* erroneously shifted towards placing unwarranted importance on how few sundries are recorded.

The primary job of a wicket-keeper is to take catches, make stumpings and play his part in run-out opportunities.

Here again we often find praise lavished on the man who, for instance, catches five and stumps two during a match as against his vis-a-vis who catches two and stumps one.

The proper comparison should of course be in regard to the chances missed.

If 'keeper A has ten chances, takes eight and misses two whilst 'keeper B has five chances and takes them all, clearly the latter has, percentage-wise, performed a more praiseworthy job. No player can take catches which are not offered.

Due regard must be paid to the one who makes chances possible by his agility or anticipation. Godfrey Evans has missed a few chances because he never shirked attempting the impossible to reach a ball. But I have seen cases where a wicket-keeper made no attempt to fly for a wide leg-side snick and in my own mind I have felt sure he wasn't prepared to risk failure.

As for sundries, these are very often caused by erratic bowling or a nasty pitch.

If a hundred runs are scored on a sticky you may be sure the wicket-keeper has been kept very busy taking some nasty flyers, whereas 500 runs on a lovely pitch may well indicate that few balls have passed the bat. It is all a question of keeping things in their proper perspective.

Lastly, the 'keeper sets the pattern for proper returns to the bowler (or nearby fieldsmen) to ensure that the bowler does not have to stoop and pick up the ball.

All of which adds up to a man-sized, responsible job. But what satisfaction at the end of a hard day to know the score sheet records no missed chances, no sundries and an indefinable contribution to the whole pattern of victory.

Running between the wickets

One of the most exhilarating experiences for a cricket spectator is to watch a partnership between two batsmen who never miss an opportunity of picking up the cheekiest of singles.

Good running is largely a matter of judgment and experience. When two great players such as Hobbs and Sutcliffe have enjoyed countless hours together at the wicket they build up a marvellous understanding and a confidence in each other which makes the task appear simple. But the hallmark of a really good runner is that he shall be able to run well with anybody. That can only be achieved by a strict observance of sound principles.

It is generally accepted that the striker is responsible for calling when the ball is hit in front of the wicket, whilst the non-striker shall call for a stroke behind the wicket. However, that must be regarded as a generalisation only. Either party must obviously have the right to deny his partner's call if he sees it is too dangerous.

Take a drive into the covers. The striker plays forward, moves into his shot and begins to advance down the pitch as fie calls. But his partner slips a trifle in starting to run and notices that cover has made rapid progress towards the ball, which is seen going to his right hand, and the signs point towards a swift return to the wicket-keeper. The non-striker thinks he has no hope of making his ground.

He would obviously be foolish to go on with the run just because theoretically it was the right thing to do, according to the textbook. He would have a duty to call "No" immediately so that not only would he be protecting himself but he would also give his partner ample time to stop and return to the crease. In such a case it is important that the denial of the striker's call must be loud, clear and prompt.

Under all circumstances initial calling, whether by striker or non-striker, should be restricted to one of three words, "yes," "no" or "wait," and every call must be decisive.

You might say, "How can the call of wait be

decisive?" Well it can be in this sense, that the other person is effectively stopped from continuing a run pending some development.

Supposing a hard cover drive is made wide of the fieldsman, who can only hope to field it one handed. Both batsmen make preliminary moves towards running, but the striker realises that a hard drive to cover is more likely to produce a run-out than one hit slowly. He therefore prefers to wait and see whether the ball is cleanly picked up or whether the fieldsman overruns it before being willing to commit himself.

Cases like this usually produce a dangerous run or an easy one, depending entirely on whether the ball is fielded cleanly.

So the value of the "wait" call in this instance is to protect the non-striker from any danger of a run-out and at the same time warn him to be at the ready should the opportunity occur to continue the run.

There are lots of ways in which the two batsmen at the wickets can help each other. Assume a ball is cut down the gully and the batsmen set off for a run. By the time they cross on the first run, the non-striker should be able to form a fairly clear judgment as to whether the stroke will yield more than a single. So on passing the striker (whose back is towards the ball) he may say, "Probably two," or some such guiding remark. This immediately gives his partner the cue to turn quickly at the end of the first run and be ready to decide immediately whether he is willing to come back towards the dangerous end for a second. The call for that second run would be the prerogative of the striker who would be returning to the wicket most likely to be endangered. The one unforgiveable sin in running is indecision. There is nothing worse than a shilly-shally in mid-pitch with neither man knowing what the other proposes to do--the sort of thing a friend of mine describes as a "perfect misunderstanding".

If in doubt say "No". Only in exceptional circumstances is one run worth the risk of a valuable wicket. After much experience with another player, expert runners can largely dispense with calling because of mutual understanding.

Pay due regard to the speed of your partner. It is essential to make sure as far as possible that each run is just as safe for him as it is for you.

That wonderful judgment of pace and distance which some men possess can be developed up to a point, though not everyone can hope to attain it. But everybody can acquire certain basic knowledge of procedure which should invariably be followed.

1. The non-striker should always backup. He does not have to stand behind the crease. So long as the bat is grounded behind, that is sufficient. I made a practice of standing outside with the bat inside as demonstrated by the photograph, and I moved off immediately I saw the ball in the air after it had left the bowler's hand.

Some players have adopted the habit of moving off as the bowler completes his run. The danger of this method is that the bowler is quite entitled to retain the ball (as his arm goes over in the delivery stride) and knock the bails off at the bowling end. If the non-striker is then out of his ground he is run-out.

Some people frown on this practice as being sharp, and think the bowler should first issue a warning. The law clearly provides that the non-striker may be run out at the bowler's end if he prematurely leaves his ground, and have seen it happen in Test cricket. Hence my dictum--watch for the ball in the air before leaving the safety zone.

2. The non-striker should always stand two or three yards wide of the return crease on the opposite side of the stumps to that from which the bowler is delivering the ball.

3. The striker should always run closer to the pitch than the non-striker. Let me make this one clearer. To a right-hand batsman, with a left-hander bowling over the wicket, the non-striker would stand on the off-side of the pitch. Should the striker play a cover drive which, by virtue of his movement, takes him over to the off-side, he too will run down that side. He should then run as close as possible to the pitch (without running on it, of course) and the non-striker should be on the outside of him. With such an understanding there is no danger of a collision or doubt about which lane to run in.

It would be wrong in such circumstances for the striker to cut across the pitch after making his shot, just in order to run down the leg side. But if he jumped down the wicket to play an on drive, he may find it easier and more convenient to continue down the on side. There can be no absolute hard-and-fast rule about which side of the pitch the striker should run. That is so often decided by circumstances. It is the non-striker's job to give his partner ample room and to protect him.

4. In making good his crease each batsman should ground his bat short of the popping crease and slide it over. This is particularly important , when attempting to avoid a run-out or when making a quick turn for a second run. There is no need for the feet to reach the crease. They may well stop a good yard short and that is ground saved. In fact, having regard to the starting position of the non-striker when he may stand outside his crease, and the distance he saves the other end, he only has to run some 18 yards.

5. As a general principle, run the first one fast in case there may be a chance of another. This must be interpreted with common sense. Plenty of shots are made where it is clearly impossible for more than one run to be scored. It would be absurd in such cases for the batsmen to wildly charge up the pitch looking for another run and merely help deplete their physical resources. On the other hand a glance to fine-leg where there is a fieldsman on the fence may well provide two runs if there is a semblance of misfielding, and the striker would need to get to the bowler's end quickly, turn and be ready for the chance,

6. Having completed a run and in the process of turning for a second, always turn towards that side of the ground on which the ball is struck. This may sound complicated but it isn't. The photographs clearly show what I mean.

A right-handed striker who makes a cover drive should, on turning for the second run, ground the bat with his left hand and turn towards cover. When making an on drive he would ground the bat with his right hand and turn towards the on side. You may think such a point is trivial. It is not. Most run-outs occur by the narrowest of margins and these refinements are the very things which make all the difference.

Good running is a joy to watch and an even greater joy to implement. Its dangers lie in slow starting and indecision. If both batsmen run immediately the ball is struck, it is amazing what they can achieve and how difficult it becomes to run them out.

And don't overlook the great value of running between wickets as an adjunct to disorganisation of an attack and a fielding plan.

So long as the covers may remain deep and short runs are not taken, so long will they enjoy the advantage of being able to cut off fours which otherwise might get through. Judicious short running may pull them in and provide major scoring opportunities.

With a left and a right-hand batsman operating together, the constant scoring of singles causes the field to change over and forces the bowler to repeatedly change his direction. No bowler Ekes that and very few can prevent it having some effect on their accuracy. Batsmen should observe which fields-men are quick, which are slow, who can throw fast, who can't, whether a man is right or left-handed, whether he is approaching the ball on his throwing side or not. There is literally no end to the subject.

Quite recently I was amused when two chaps were going for a run and the striker called out so loudly we heard him in the pavilion, "Come two--he has a glass arm." The same result could have been achieved without embarrassing the fieldsman and revealing to the fielding captain what he had observed.

Even though a run-out appears inevitable, never give up. Many a batsman has made his ground safely because the wicket-keeper, in his excitement over a chance, has fumbled the ball, or when the fieldsman has failed to gather cleanly or thrown wildly in his urgent attempt to beat the batsman. If you give up the chase, you give added time and confidence to the fielding side who are less likely then to fall into error.

Should you accidentally drop the bat in running, it is mostly quicker to keep going than to stop and retrieve it. The bat can be safely picked up after the run is completed.

Despite every precaution run-outs will occur. More often than not no doubt exists as to who is to be the victim. But occasionally, through a misunderstanding, both batsmen find themselves in the middle and a run-out for somebody is inevitable.

If one of them is a recognised first-class bat and the other a rabbit, the latter should immediately sacrifice his own wicket by making certain he gets into the position which ensures he gets trapped. That is one of the rare cases where, in the interests of the team, the better batsman has a right to be selfish and allow his partner to be sacrificed.

Finally, don't forget to learn the rule about a substitute runner. You never know when (a) you may need one or (b) when your partner may need one and you will have to run with him. It would be a pity if you were run-out simply because you didn't realise that when striking, both you and your substitute are vulnerable. The striker may be out stumped or run-out even though his substitute runner is behind the crease. And the striker may be out if his substitute is guilty of "handling the ball" or "obstructing the field".

10

CAPTAINCY

The captain of the cricket team is the person who more than any other can influence the enjoyment of the game for both player and spectator alike. More than that, the captain can be responsible for the atmosphere within the club as a whole. It is a position of importance and responsibility and whoever takes on the role must be aware of these things and not enter into the position lightly. Cricket is all to do with the enjoyment of a sporting environment which will set standards of behaviour both on and off the field and will encourage all those that play to improve their performance, not only to give pleasure to themselves, but more importantly, to others. With this in mind, the good captain will lead the team in a manner that will earn their respect, as this is the only way it can be attained. Winning must be the ultimate of any captain, but not winning at all costs. The game is worth more than this, and there is no disgrace in trying your utmost to avoid defeat once the chance of victory has gone. If you can cultivate an optimistic, but realistic attitude, your job as captain will be that much easier. The majority of people thrive on encouragement and an optimistic word from the captain can work wonders. This applies equally to the experienced campaigner or the club's newest and youngest member. Do not feel that you have necessarily got to lead from the front, by scoring all the runs, taking all the wickets and generally trying to be everything to everybody. Teams like to be proud of their captain and their pride must come from the manner in which you behave, whether it be in your unselfish manner or your impartiality, your good manners or in the way you pass on your wide knowledge of the game. The way that you perform is also important, not so much in number of runs or wickets, but more in your appreciation of the game as it stands. If there is an example for you to set, it must be by your effort in the field. Discipline is important in a team, particularly on tour. Anyone can play a bad shot or drop a catch and neither warrants a sour-tongued comment in public from the caption.

There can be no excuse for bad sportsmanship from a player and the captain should make everyone aware of this. Only take a player to task in front of the team if all else has failed and after repeated attempts in private. There will be times when you can do no wrong, and on those occasions you can easily feel indispensable for ever. Equally, your world can be very bleak when all your plans go wrong and winning a match or scoring a run is a distant memory. It is on these days that your mark is left, for after all, you can only be the temporary representative of those who appoint you.

On winning the toss

Many are the captains that have been labelled "genius" or "hopeless" by the uninformed, simply on the strength of their luck with the toss. "Win the toss and win the match" the saying goes and in many instances this is true. How can the toss of a coin have such an influence on the game?

Many factors can influence a captain's decision to bat or field on winning the toss. In general, the shorter the time allocated to a match, the less the conditions of play (i.e. the playing surface and atmosphere) will change and the more the decision to bat or field will be psychological and dependent on the captain's knowledge of his team's strengths and weaknesses. Some teams perform better chasing a total; other teams prefer to have their runs on the board. Sometimes, in club and schools cricket, when only one new ball is used in a match, a captain with a strong pace attack may choose to field first on winning the toss, to give his opening bowlers the advantage of the new ball. If the "boot is on the other foot" and the opposition have a strong pace attack capable of using the new ball to advantage, the captain must again give serious consideration to fielding first.

As the time allocated to a match increases, so does the importance attached to winning the toss. A psychological factor that applies to all forms of cricket and tempts the captain to bat first is the theory that in a tense situation (usually the last innings) a bowler is less affected by pressure than a batsman. Fortunately for the game, this is only a theory and is certainly not always the case. However, it will be appreciated that a batsman, realising that he can normally only afford one mistake, will feel more pressure than a bowler who usually has the luxury of another chance, should he make a mistake.

Having commented on the psychological aspects of winning the toss and batting or fielding, it is fair to say that in matches of one day and more changing playing conditions, mainly caused by weather, have the greater influence on the result. For example, when the playing surface is dry at the commencement of the match, the team batting first can usually expect the best of the batting conditions. That is, the pitch can only get worse through the effect of wear or rain. More often than not, a cricket pitch will increasingly help the spin bowler the longer the match progresses. The amount of grass on a pitch can also influence its behaviour. Very often a well grassed pitch will suit the pace bowlers. In these circumstances a captain can be tempted to put the opposing team in to bat on winning the toss. This is an infrequent occurence, however, and is only usually done when in addition to the pitch being "grassy", it is also wet and drying quickly, either through wind or sun. Captains should be most careful in their assessment of a wet pitch, as only when it is drying quickly can the decision to bowl first be completely justified, regardless of whether the pitch is well grassed or not.

In discussing the playing surface so far, we have considered only the pitch or the wicket, whichever one prefers to call it. In fact, the conditions of the out-field should be noted by the captain, as this can be a significant factor in his decision on winning the toss. For example, if a team have to bat on a slow, wet out-field after having fielded on a fast, dry out-field, they will be at an obvious disadvantage -- a fact that should not be underrated. Remember also that a wet ball severely hampers all types of bowler, as does a slippery, wet runup.

When looking to the weather as a guide to how it

may affect the playing surface, well before and at the commencement of a match, the captain should also be aware of how the weather may affect the atmosphere. A heavy overcast sky will assist the pace bowlers, as will a humid atmosphere, causing the ball to swing more than it would normally do. Whilst this may not be a strong reason for bowling first (the overcast sky may forecast rain), it is something to be taken into consideration when making the final decision. And so even with the knowledge and more, contained in the preceding notes, a famous Yorkshire and England captain once said: "If you win the toss and think about fielding first, think about it as much as you want, but make sure your team bat first". Whilst one need not be quite so dogmatic, reasonable advice to a captain would be—if in doubt, bat! Fortunately, cricket, being the game it is, confounds the best laid plans and both the best and worst captains have a happy knack of winning against the odds. "A good toss to lose" is a quote I have heard somewhere.

On fielding

Up to actually tossing the coin with the opposing captain, there is generally little urgency as players change and sometimes practise, either on instructions or not. Once the toss has decided your fate, however, there is a definite change in the dressing-room atmosphere and tempo. When the team is in the field, there is a more collective urgency, even if the batsman who had been mentally preparing to bat do tend to relax. This is the time when the captain has a very important part to play. In the time remaining before leading the team out into the field, you must wear a number of different caps. It may be necessary to give me team a "pep talk", maybe highlighting one or two outstanding tactical points. The team's different personalities will need to be treated quite differently, lifting some players and calming others. Some thought will have to be given to the prevailing conditions, both of the ground and the atmosphere. Which direction is the wind blowing? Is last night's rain going to affect the pitch? Is our star fast bowler really fit? A host of other thoughts will cross your mind before someone says "the umpires have gone skipper".

The good captain will, of course, have done a considerable amount of pre-match planning. Everyone in the team will know exactly where he is fielding; both opening bowlers will have warmed up and be ready to bowl "flat out" from the start. The opposing batsmen will have been discussed and everyone will be aware of the plan of attack.

In the first over or two, adjustments may have to be made in the actual positions, as the pace of the wicket and the outfield determine the angles and speed of the ball leaving the bat. Throughout the innings, the captain will be checking the exact positions of all the fielders and they in turn should be watching the captain for instructions when the ball is dead. Constant contact, discussion, and encouragement for the bowlers will be a prime consideration. It will be particularly important for the captain to keep in touch with the bowlers who are not in action at the time. This will encourage them and make them feel a part of the game. The wicket-keeper can be a valuable ally in the field and a vital supporting influence to the captain. Everyone in the field should be in no doubt as to who is in charge and the captain will need to assert his authority on occasions, sometimes through controversial bowling or field placing changes. In fact, it is most important that a captain uses imagination and does not become predictable.

At the same time, common sense must prevail, particularly in the handling of bowlers. For example, the captain will, or should, know whether a wicket is taking spin or helping the pace bowler. Whichever, he should back his judgment at all times. If a spin bowler is in the team, he should bowl on a spinner's wicket, regardless of the fact that an outstanding fast bowler is in the team. Only in this way can bowlers develop their skills. Captains should take care not to over-bowl their main bowlers when conditions are in their favour. Many is the time I have seen a marvellous early performance on a "green wicket" by the main strike bowlers, only to see them "run out of steam" through being over-bowled in their first spell. It is a temptation that must be resisted and a strong reminder on the necessity of really knowing your bowlers' capabilities.

The hallmark of the really astute captain is in his assessment of the opposition and how any knowledge he has is used. The clever captain in the field will ensure that his bowlers' best efforts are concentrated on exerting pressure on the weaker of the two batsmen at the wicket. The whole team must be made aware of the importance of saving singles, especially when the stronger batsman is intent on retaining the strike. This is particularly important towards ~he end of an innings, when the difference in the abilities of the batsmen at the wicket is more obvious. Good captains are aware of the importance of not wasting time in the field. Different placings for different batsmen should be established without exaggerated discussions.

Field placing

Captains worthy of their name should make a study of field placing. It can be the most significant aspect in the success of their team. Here are a few pointers:

1. Study the style and temperament of each batsman who comes to the wicket. If possible, have previous knowledge of his style of play. Take immediate advantage of this knowledge and set your field accordingly.
2. Know as much as you can about the ground on which you are playing and how it tends to play in different weather conditions.
3. Know the opposing captain and his style of play.
4. Brief your team well as to the strengths and weaknesses of the opposition.
5. Recognise your own strengths. For example, do not set ultra attacking fields when you know your bowling will not stand it. Nothing gives the opposition greater heart than a really fast start to their innings.
6. The captain has the final authority on the placing of the field, but the best captains cooperate with their bowlers. In fact, the experienced bowler is usually given first option as to where exactly he wants his field.
7. Knowing all the circumstances, be exact in your field placings without wasting time. There is no need for it in a well-briefed team. If different field

placings are required for different batsmen, the field should change quickly as the bowler moves back to his mark. Let your field ebb and flow with the state of the game. Never let it stagnate.

8. Remember, you cannot set afield forbad bowling.
9. If a fielder drops a catch or misfields a ball, a word of commiseration and encouragement will help him next time a chance comes his way. An angry word or gesture will do no good for anyone.

Field placing diagrams for different bowlers are included at the end of the chapter on Bowling and a general diagram, showing all the fielding positions, is included in the chapter on Fielding.

On batting

There is an entirely different role for the captain to play when his team is batting, depending very much on whether it is the first innings or whether they are chasing a total set by the opposition. Invariably to begin with, he is looking for the early batsmen to set up a reasonable total as a platform from which to attack the bowling later. This will apply even when chasing a total against the clock. There is nothing like wickets in hand to give batsmen the incentive to play their strokes freely. The captain will, of course, have influenced team selection, from which he will have planned the normal batting order in advance. If possible, a left-handed batsman will be included in the first three or four. This causes the bowlers to constantly be changing their line of attack, having an unsettling effect on the inexperienced bowler. If one of the opening batsmen can be a stroke-maker of high quality, so much the better. If he is successful, the pressure is so much less on the later batsmen. The captain himself should be at least a capable batsman, enabling him to set a sound example and occasionally play an innings of note. Running between wickets is a very important part of the team batting effort and the captain should always be looking to set an example in this.

Occasionally, it may be necessary to change the batting order for tactical purposes. I do not feel this is done enough in all types of cricket. Neither is enough serious batting practice and coaching given to tail-end batsmen. This is hard to believe in hindsight and yet we still expect numbers ten and eleven to bat like masters in a crisis. It is very important that the whole team know exactly what is required of each of them whenever they go in to bat. The batsman who does not play to the captain's instructions in the interests of the team, should always be disciplined to the extent of omitting him from the next match or two if necessary. Everyone, including the captain, should be aware that cricketers everywhere will acknowledge that the game will always be greater than the player.

After the match

This is the time when winning and losing is forgotten and both captains and teams get together, even if only briefly. The real cricketers will have been modest in victory and congratulatory in defeat. It is a time for captains to acknowledge the work put in by so many people behind the scenes; the groundsmen, the umpires, the ladies who so willingly make meals and so often play such an important part in the life of a club, the scorers, and many more without whom the game would not be the same. It certainly is not a time for recrimination, but for those who have not done so well in the game, a quiet word of encouragement for the future will make up for everything.

Later, when the players have departed, or as soon as possible in the days ahead, the captain should look back on the game objectively, thinking on what lessons he may have learned for the future and how he may improve his own performance next time. He must make a mental note of how he may help players in the practice sessions before the next match, and if the team have played away from home, it can be a nice idea to "drop a line" to those whose hospitality the team and himself have enjoyed.

Circumstances quite naturally decree that few men get the opportunity to captain an international cricket team. It is the highest honour which the game has to bestow and it entails heavy responsibility. The leadership on the field is important but there are many other ways too in which the captain's influence and example are vital.

It is essential that a captain should enjoy the respect and confidence of his team. Not only must his cricket record be such that he is looked up to as a player but also his private life must be beyond reproach.

When the captain is bent on a good time, his team mates quickly find out and there is a resultant deterioration in morale and discipline. But when the boys know their skipper is literally wearing himself out for their sakes and that of the game, they will strive to the utmost, even when disagreeing with his decisions. Loyalty, built upon admiration and respect, is a powerful force.

A good captain must be a fighter: confident but not arrogant, firm but not obstinate, able to take criticism without letting it unduly disturb him, for he is sure to get it--and unjustly too. It is customary for cricket teams to be chosen by a selection committee, but the controlling administrative authority normally reserves the right to veto the selection of any player on grounds other than cricket ability. This shows that sheer sporting prowess is not regarded as the sole qualification for a player.

In the early days of international cricket it is understandable that the demands on a captain were not so heavy as they are now. The mode of travel was more leisurely, and newspapers did not devote anything like the space to reporting matches and the movements of players as they do today. In fact that state of affairs was true in some measure up to the start of the first World War.

Things gradually changed in the 1920's. The advent of moving pictures was followed by the sound film and the newsreel theatre. Then came radio and the introduction of ball-by-ball broadcasts. The day of the specialist cricket reporter arrived. Instead of a few regular newspaper men covering a Test match, the number has grown into a small army.

Now we have television and it would be a brave man who could forecast what further miracle of scientific invention may come along to cast its impact on the game,

Television is at once the most wonderful and fearsome creation. It not only takes the spoken word into the homes of millions but it portrays so vividly, with the telephoto lens, every action and gesture of a player. No longer can anyone feel secure that a momentary outburst of temper or feeling will remain unobserved.

There has already been a claim that expert lip readers can tell the innermost thoughts of a batsman who mutters under his breath some unprintable epithet. The insidious part of television is that the subject may not be aware he is being televised.

The strain of this constant glare of publicity is bad enough for the average player, For the captain it is far worse.

International tours are acknowledged as having considerable political significance and players have been awarded honours because of their contribution to the cause of mutual understanding and goodwill between nations. International leadership can only come as a result of apprenticeship in lower grades, and any player who aspires to such a position, or who realises he may be destined for it, should use these formative years to the best advantage in acquiring the knowledge which will stand him in good stead later on.

It is impossible to manufacture an ideal captain or to lay down precise qualifications for one. However, as a general principle I think it is far easier for a specialist batsman to handle the position than a bowler, an all-rounder or a wicket-keeper.

The difficulty with a bowler is the constant fear that he will bowl himself too much and thereby incur an undercurrent of dissatisfaction amongst his colleagues, or underbowl himself because of undue modesty. Moreover, preoccupation with his personal responsibilities on the field makes it difficult for him to exercise the same critical observation of all details which a batsman can.

A wicket-keeper suffers from the disability that he must minutely concentrate on every ball, even from the moment the bowler's run commences. Adding to that burden the task of captaincy is really too much. It does not matter in fixtures of lesser importance, but I think it is an unfair responsibility in the international field.

A great captain does not have to be his team's finest player. Nevertheless it must be to his advantage that his selection is in no doubt. The man who is not sure of his position can scarcely have that freedom of mind which a captain needs. And the man who has the ability to uplift and inspire his colleagues by performance on the field must have an advantage providing, of course, other qualifications are equal. It is the sum total of effort which thousands of club cricket captains put into their jobs which does so much towards moulding the outlook of the average cricketer. Their influence for good or evil on this great game is incalculable. The public see what happens on the field and largely form their judgment by such observation or even on performance.

One of England's most successful county captains is reputed to have said, "The public are not interested in the team which runs second." That may have been a harsh verdict but it is not without truth. Even so, the words were possibly spoken more with a purpose in mind than with a regard to strict accuracy. The captain was trying to instil into his men that their job was to win, not play for a draw.

One must applaud such a motive. Cricket needs initiative and enterprise from its leaders. These attributes are the very core of attractive play, and one of the greatest dangers to cricket is that so many matches drift along to a stage when they become boring to everybody. It is not enough to try to win matches towards the end. The same spirit should be evident from the commencement.

There were plenty of occasions when we were outplayed. Sometimes we had to be content with or even fight desperately to achieve a draw. But only once can deliberately allowing a match to drift into a draw. It was the fourth Test at Adelaide in 1947. Australia held the Ashes and were leading two to nil in the series. We only had to make a draw of this particular game to win the rubber and retain "The Ashes".

From the outset we tried to win but on the last day the position was that England were 247 runs ahead and had two wickets in hand. With Compton and Evans at the wickets, the former, being the No. 1 batsman, tried to keep the strike. Evans refused to run for his own shots late in the over so that Compton would have the bowling as much as possible. The situation was such that Evans batted 135 minutes for ten runs. England, of course, wanted us to make a present of quick runs to Compton so that they might have time to dismiss us later in the day.

We refused to allow the initiative to be taken from me in this way and, therefore, deliberately kept a deep field and held the scoring rate down. If England were not prepared to take a risk, why should present them with a chance to win, having regard to the state of the rubber.

The match petered out in a rather dismal fashion and I fear the spectators obtained poor entertainment, for which I was extremely sorry, but I felt England should take the initiative to try to win. It wasn't my job to do so on that occasion.

These unfortunate situations arise occasionally but how much better to see both sides striving for a result.

A captain must use judgment as to how long it is to be maintained or whether, in fact, it is justified at all.

I'm afraid so many opening batsmen are defensive minded that it nearly always pays. Defensive batting is always best against the close field when the ball is new. As a captain, one would prefer to see their opening batsmen prepared and willing to play shots unless forced on the defensive. When fieldsmen are close to the bat they have to be rather exceptional to cope with full-blooded shots. They are there to catch snicks and mis-hits or defensive prods.

So, whilst approving attacking fields, we don't think captains are enterprising enough in combating them. Instructions to opening batsmen to take advantage of no outfields would probably disperse many of these fields quicker and more successfully than is the case today. The "occupancy of the crease" theory can become a curse. It is frequently an excuse propounded by those deplorable batsmen who seek to improve their batting averages at the expense of attractive cricket and their team's welfare. Captains should be very firm in instructing players to carry out their policy.

Much of a captain's best work is done in the

dressing-room, at the practice nets or at least off the field of play. The arena is where one sees the culmination of his planning. One thing strongly advocate is that all captains should thoroughly study and understand the laws of cricket. They are fascinating and will repay the time spent on them.

The history of cricket, its whole background and evolution, traditions and so on can be gleaned from the marvellous volumes which have been handed down to us by historians, cricketers, statisticians, etc. Every prospective international captain should be an avid reader. Not only will it help him on the field but he may find that his counsel and guidance are sought in the conference room regarding the future development of cricket.

It is astonishing how many great players make no effort to enlarge their knowledge. They are the losers. How many men have you heard say that they don't believe in interfering with the laws of the game. They don't really know what they are talking about. If taken literally they mean we should still be using curved bats and have two stumps, two feet apart so that the ball could pass between.

The young player is only emulating when he looks at a photograph great player of an earlier generation says, "How could he be any good with a stance like that," or some equally cutting observation. How much better if he could, very early in life, extract the virtues of the methods of previous generations and adapt them to modem ones. The captain, most of all, can get things in better perspective by a thorough knowledge of history.

The problems on the field of play involve judgment and experience. At the very outset a captain may win the toss and be faced with the decision whether to bat or not. If it is a Test match, he will probably bat. The pitch is usually at its best on the first day, there are perhaps three or four days to go in which the vagaries of the weather are more likely to help the side which bats first than their opponents, and the game is sudden death.

A county match may be quite different. The question of points at the end of the season can dictate the policy.

Assuming the team winning the toss has a very strong bowling side and must win (a draw being no use) to keep them in the fight, the captain may well take the risk and give his opponents first knock to obviate any danger of having runs to spare at the end. Here is an example of how circumstances can work out. Team A wins the toss and bats, making 300. Team B makes 200. Team A bats a second time and the captain declares at 200 for five, leaving B 300 to get. At stumps on the last day team B is 140 for nine. Match drawn. In that case 160 runs are available to cover the last wicket and time has saved the side.

If team B batted first and made 200 and say 150 (all out) second innings, Team A could well have won the match with two or three hours to spare.

These sort of long-range calculations must sometimes be considered by the captain before committing himself to bat or not. A wrong decision then may involve the danger of a tricky declaration later on.

Credit is seldom given to the wise move which smoothes the later path.

This question of deciding in advance how a wicket will play is not an easy one. After years of experience one can easily be trapped, and sure that even some groundsmen don't know what will happen before the first ball is bowled. One has to consider the nature and hardness of the soil, the quantity and type of grass, the amount of moisture in the pitch, the atmosphere (whether the day is hot and dry or dull and humid) and so on. And nature has a nasty habit of altering her mind about what she will do after the captain makes his decision.

The critics always adjudicate after they see what did happen but the unfortunate captain is given no such licence. He is so often judged by the result, not the wisdom of a decision.

Quite recently a young captain having his first season in that capacity won the toss and sent his opponents in to bat. The results were not what he had expected and he was rather severely criticised. Naturally he was somewhat perturbed but reminded him that history so often records its verdict according to the result of an action and not according to whether it was correct by all the known factors. Remember the unfortunate English captain who sent Australia in to bat at Leeds after he won the toss? Bardsley was caught first ball. Macartney gave a slips catch off the fifth but it was dropped, and he proceeded to make a century before lunch. The skipper was in trouble. But what if that slip catch had been held? He might have been a hero. You see it wasn't his decision that mattered, it was the result.

A captain is often faced with the question of when to take a new ball. At 5.30, his fast bowlers tired and two men well set, he may prefer to wait until tomorrow. Or should he? The batting order, unless agreed by prior arrangement with the selectors, can often be much more important than is generally realised. I am a great believer in having set positions for players. It is better that the openers know their job and are accustomed to it, and that other players get into the regular habit of going in No. 3, 4, etc.

Circumstances inevitably dictate a change now and again, but as a general rule I am in no doubt that the alteration of a regular batting order tends to be disturbing to the individual. In addition to the players personal habit it has the virtue of allowing the same fellows to bat together more often and so get accustomed to their methods of running between wickets. It also enables the building up of a regular policy such as having an enterprising attacking player in a certain position, a left-hander at say No. 5, and so on.

Openers must possess a sound defence but think at least one of them should be capable of aggressive batsmanship. To start on the defensive so early seldom pays dividends. It is the policy of a draw and cricket is first and foremost a game to be won.

Whilst captains should not have to bother themselves about the small routine things, they are nevertheless responsible. The rules for instance lay down a maximum of two minutes between batsmen. Some players seem to think this time must be taken, and have often noticed the incoming batsman standing at the entrance gate waiting until the dismissed player has left the arena before he enters. This, of course, is unnecessary and a captain should make it clear to his team that he wishes each new batsman to take his place at the crease as soon as possible. The sum of these small matters adds greatly to public entertainment.

Circumstances may arise whereby a captain does the right thing by prolonging a match. If the result is a foregone conclusion he may do his team a major service by resting his regular bowlers and entrusting the dismissal of the opponents to less experienced men.

When to close an innings sometimes presents a tricky problem. Fine judgment must often be exercised. The risk of losing must be balanced against the possibility of a win--the time factor being all important. Due appraisal must be made of the relative skills of the two teams. Whether a wicket will be easier or more difficult with the passage of time, e.g., a wet wicket under the influence of sun.

England lost one Test against Australia because the closure was delayed too long. England badly wanted runs and the skipper was reluctant to close. But the extra runs he gained in the last half-hour were as nothing alongside the wickets he might have taken on that sticky dog. As it was the pitch dried out over the week-end, we made a big score and won.

There are captains who overwork their fast bowlers at the start of play and ruin them for the day. Others take them off by the clock even though meeting with success. It is a great mistake to tire a fast bowler out in one long spell. He seldom recaptures his zip that day. The only time it is justified is when the captain feels he has a major prize within his grasp if he can push home an early advantage and is willing to risk using his bowler right up.

Reasonably quick bowling changes are normally sound policy. Any change at all may cause the batsman to fall into error just because of the difference in pace, flight, etc.--not necessarily because the change bowls any better.

One of the greatest arts of captaincy is in being able to anticipate a batsman's weak spot. How often do we see a player spoon the ball in a certain place and immediately a fieldsman is placed there. Seldom does a second chance occur because the batsman has been warned.

If only the captain could sense it coming and have his fieldsman there the first time. When a bowler is a fully experienced international with a set type of field he may not need any help, but for a young bowler just entering big cricket, nothing can ruin him quicker than bad field placing which enables fours to be hit at random. The bowler becomes demoralised--thinks lie is no good and loses all confidence.

An intelligent captain who will give him a sensible protective field and save him from punishment, who will advise him and know just how and when to use him, can do much towards deciding his future career.

At all times the captain should set the pattern, take his team into his confidence and let them know where they are going. One captain who would sit in a corner of the dressing-room and refuse to watch his team batting. How he was able to intelligently direct his batting from such a position. It is the sort of attitude which stems from a stupid childish superstition.

A discussion between a captain and his men during the progress of play can often prove helpful. The bowler's strategy may be pinpointed or ideas put forward which will help later batsmen. No captain has so much knowledge that he cannot profit by listening to others, and he is a wise man who will consult senior colleagues occasionally. The wicket-keeper in particular is often in a position to pass on valuable hints.

There are so many ways in which a captain must be constantly thinking.

Whether the field placing is just right.

Whether the bowler needs a spell.

Whether the pitch calls for a different type of bowler.

There is virtually no end to the problems.

How right was Sir Frederick Toone when he said, "Cricket is a science, the study of a lifetime, in which you may exhaust yourself but never your subject."

11

RULES AND REGULATIONS

The Hambeldon Club was founded in about 1750 and played a significant part in the evolution of game. It was superseded by the Marylebone Cricket Club, with its headquarters at Lords, London. This became the world authority of the sport and its sanctuary. In 1873, the official county championships began in England and it became International Game with the formation of the Imperial Cricket Conference in 1909. Australia and England used to play friendly matches but the first official test match was played between the two countries in 1877. Most famous of all cricket terms is the 'the Ashes'. Its origin goes back to an historical match between England and Australia played at the Oval in London in 1882. The Englishmen thoroughly beaten and, in, fact, the test had been so exciting that one of the spectators dropped dead.

Cricket was brought to Indian subcontinent by the British. There are references to cricket having been played in Indian in the early parts of the 18th century. In the beginning the game was played amongst the Britishers. By the beginning the 19th century, the local population also started taking interest in the game particularly in the cities of Bombay, Calcutta and Madras. When the Indian princes evinced a keen interest in the game, the sport really caught the imagination of the Indians and soon they started making rapid progress in the game and in 1886 a Parsi team toured England, the visit being returned in 1888-89. The presidency matches began in 1892-93 between Parsis and Europeans and the tournament became the Bombay Triangular, with the Hindus fielding a team in 1907-08. In 1912-13, the tournament became quadrangular with the entry of Muslims in the field. With the efforts of several Princes, H.E Grant-Goven and A S de Mellow, the national championship the Ranji Trophy began in 1935.

India played its first official Test against England and in 1932 and has since played nearly 1954 officials tests against Australia, England, Pakistan, New Zealand and West Indies.

The players

Number of players and Captain: A match is played between two sides each of eleven player's, one of whom shall be Captain. In the event of the Captain not being available at any time a Deputy shall act for him.

Nomination of players: Before the toss for innings, the Captain shall nominate his players who may not there after be changed without the consent of the opposing Captain.

Substitutes and runners

Substitutes: In normal circumstances, a substitute shall be allowed to field only for a player who satisfies the Umpires that he had become injured or become ill during the match. However, in very exceptional circumstances, the Umpires may use their discretion to allow a substitute for a player who has to leave the field or does not take the field for other wholly acceptable reasons, subject to consent being given by the opposing Captain. If a player wishes to change his shirt, boots, etc. He may leave the field to do so (no changing on the field) but no substitute will be allowed. The opposing Captain shall have no right of objection to any player acting as substitute in the field, nor as to where he shall field, although he may object to the substitute acting as Wicket-Keeper. A substitute shall not be allowed to bat or bowl. A player may bat, bowl or field even though a substitute has acted for him.

Runner: A Runner shall be allowed for a batsman who during the match is incapacitated by illness or injury. The player acting as Runner shall be member of the batting side and shall, if possible, have already batted in that innings. The player acting as Runner for an injured Batsman shall wear the same external protective equipment as the injured Batsman.

Fieldman leaving the field: No Fieldman shall leave the field or return during a session of play without the consent of the Umpire at the Bowler's end. The Umpire's consent is also necessary if a Substitute is required for a Fieldsman, when his side returns to the field after an interval. If a member of the fielding side leaves the field or fails to return after an interval and is absent from the field for longer than 15 minutes, he shall not be permitted to bowl after his return until he has been on the field for at least that length of playing time for which he was absent. This restriction shall not apply at the start of a new day's play.

Batsman leaving the field or retiring: A Batsman may leave the field or retire at any time owing to illness, injury or other unavoidable cause, having previously notified the Umpire at the Bowler's end. He may resume his innings at the fall of a wicket, which for the purposes of his Law shall include the retirement of another Batsman. If he leaves the field or retires for any other reason he may only resume his innings with the consent of the opposing Captain. When a Batsman has left the field or retired and is unable to return owing to illness, injury or other unavoidable cause, his innings is to be recorded as "retired, not out". Otherwise it is to be recorded as "retired, out".

Commencement of a batsman's innings: A Batsman shall be considered to have commenced his innings once he has stepped on to the field of play.

The umpires

Before the toss for innings two Umpires shall be appointed, one for each end, to control the game with absolute impartiality as required by the Laws. No Umpire shall be changed during a match without the consent of both Captains.

The scorers

All runs scored shall be recorded by scorers appointed for the purpose. Where there are two Scorers they shall frequently check to ensure that the score sheets agree. The Scorers shall accept and immediately acknowledge all instructions and signals given to them by the Umpires.

The ball

The ball, when new, shall weigh not less than 5 ounces 155.9 g.nor more than 5¾ ounces/163 g: and shall measure not less than 8.13/16 inches/22.4cm., nor more than 9 inches/22.9 cm. in circumference. All balls used in matches shall be approved by the Umpires and Captains before the start of the match. Subject to agreement to the contrary, having been made before he toss, either Captain may demand a new ball at the start of each innings. In a match of 3 or more days duration, the Captain of the fielding side may demand a new ball after the prescribed number of overs has been bowled with the old one. The Governing body for cricket in the country concerned shall decide the number of overs applicable in that country which shall be not less than 75 six-ball over (55 eight-ball overs). In the event of a ball during play being lost or, in the opinion of the Umpires, becoming unfit for play, the Umpires shall allow it to be replaced by one that in their opinion has had a similar amount of wear. If a ball is to be replaced, the Umpires shall inform the Batsmen.

The bat

The bat overall shall not be more than 38 inches/96.5 cm in length; the blade of the bat shall be made of wood and shall not exceed 4/1/4 inches/10.8 cm at the widest part.

The pitch

The pitch is the area between the bowling creases. It shall measure 5 ft./1.52m. in width on either side of a line joining the centre of the middle stumps of the wicket.

Before the toss for inning, the Executive of the thereafter the Umpires shall control its use and maintenance. The pitch shall not be changed during a match unless becomes unfit for play, and then only with the consent of both Captains. In the event of a non-turf pitch being used, the following shall apply:

(a) Length: That of the playing surface to a minimum of 58 ft. (17.68 m)

(b) Width: That of the playing surface to a minimum of 6 ft. (1.83 m)

The wickets

Two sets of wickets, each 9 inches/22.86 cm. Wide, and consisting of the three wooden stumps with two wooden bails upon the top, shall be pitched opposite and parallel to each other at a distance of 22 yards/ 20.12 m. between the centres of the two middle stumps. The stumps shall be of equal and sufficient size to prevent the ball from passing between them. Their tops shall be 28 inches/71.1 cm. above the ground, and shall be dome-shaped except for the bail grooves. The balls shall be each 4 3/8 inches/11.1 cm. in length and when in position on the top of the stumps shall not project more than ½ inch 1.3 cm. above them.

The bowling, popping and return creases

he bowling crease shall be marked in line with the stumps at each end shall be 8 ft. 8 inches/2.64 m. in length, with the stumps in the centre. The popping crease, which is the back edge of the crease marking, shall be in front of and parallel with the bowling crease. It shall have the back edge of the crease marking 4 ft/1.22 m. from the centre of the stumps and shall be considered to be unlimited in length. A forward extension shall be marking to the popping crease.

During the match the pitch may be rolled at the request of the Captain of the batting side, for a period of not more than 7 minutes before the start of each day's play. In addition, if after the toss and before the first innings of the much, the start is delayed, the Captain of the batting side shall have the right to have the pitch rolled for not more than 7 minutes. The pitch shall not otherwise be rolled during the match. The 7 minutes rolling permitted before the start of a day's play shall take place not earlier than half an hour before, the start of play and the captain of the batting side may delay such rolling unit 10 minutes before the start of play should he so desire. If a captain declares an innings closed less than 15 minutes before the resumption of play, and the other captain is thereby prevented from exercising his option of 7 minutes rolling or if he is so prevented for any other reason the time for rolling shall be taken out the normal playing time. Sweeping of the pitch as is necessary during the match shall be done so that the 7 minutes allowed for rolling the pitch provided for in 1. above is not affected.

Mowing:

(a) Responsibilities of ground authority and of umpires: All mowing which are carried out before the toss for innings shall be the responsibility of the Ground Authority. Thereafter they shall be carried out under the supervision of the Umpires.

(b) Initial mowing: The pitch shall be mown before play begins on the day the match is scheduled to start or in the case of a delayed start on the day the match is expected to start.

(c) Subsequent mowing in a Match of 2 or more day's duration: In a match of two or more day's duration, the pitch shall be mown daily before play begins. Should this mowing not take place because of weather conditions, rest days or other reasons the pitch shall be mown on the first day on which the match is resumed.

(d) Mowing of the outfield in a Match day's duration: In order to ensure that conditions are as similar as possible for both sides, the outfield shall normally be mown before the commencement of play on each day of the match, if ground and weather conditions allow.

The pitch shall not be watered during a match. Whenever possible the creases shall be re-marked. In wet weather, the Umpires shall ensure that the holes made by the Bowlers and Batsmen are cleaned out and dried whenever necessary to facilitate play. In matches of 2 or more days's duration, the Umpires shall allow, if necessary, the re-turfing of foot holes made by the Bowler in his delivery stride, or the use of quick-setting fillings for the same purpose, before the start of each day's play. During play, the Umpire shall allow either Batsman to beat the pitch with his bat and players to secure their footholds by the use of sawdust, provided that no damage to the pitch is so caused is not contravened.

Covering the pitch before the start of a Match

Before the start of a match complete covering of the pitch shall be allowed. The pitch shall not be completely covered during a match unless prior arrangement crease.

Innings

A match shall be of one or two innings of each side according to agreement reached before the start of play. In a two innings match each side shall take their innings alternately. The captains shall toss for the choice of innings on the field of play not later than 15 minutes before the time scheduled for the match to start, or before the time agree upon for play to start.

The winner of the toss shall notify his decision to bat or to field to the opposing captain not later than 10 minutes before the time scheduled for the march to start, or before the time agreed upon for play to start. The decision shall not thereafter be altered. Despite the terms of 1. above, in a one innings match, when a result has been reached on the first innings the Captains may agree to the continuation of play if, in their opinion, there is a prospect of carrying the game to a further issue in the time left.

The follow-on

In a two innings match the side which bats first and leads by 200 runs in a match of five days or more, by 150 runs in a three-day or four-day match, by 100 runs in a two-day match, or by 75 runs in a one-day match, shall have the option of requiring the other side to follow their innings.

If no play take place on the first day of a match of 2 or more day's duration, 1. above shall apply in accordance with the number of day's play remaining from the actual start of the match.

Declarations

The Captain of the batting side may declare an innings closed at any time during a match irrespective of its duration. A Captain may forfeit his second innings, provided his decision to do so is notified to the opposing Captain and Umpires in sufficient time to allow 7 minutes rolling of the pitch. The normal 10 minute interval between innings shall be applied.

Start of play

At the start of each innings and of each day's play and on the resumption of play after any interval or interruption the Umpire at the Bowlers' end shall call "play". At no time on any day of the match shall there be any bowling or batting practice on the pitch. No practice may take place on the field if, in the opinion of the Umpires, it could result in a waste of time.

Trial Run-Up: No Bowler shall have a trial run-up after "play" has been called in any session of play, except at the fall of a wicket when an Umpire may allow such a trial run-up if he is satisfied that it will not cause waste of time.

Intervals

The Umpire shall allow such intervals as have been agreed upon for meals, and 10 minutes between each innings. If an innings ends or there is a stoppage caused by weather or bad light within 10 minutes of the agreed time for the luncheon interval, the interval shall be taken immediately. The time remaining in the session of play shall be added to the agreed length of the interval but no extra allowance shall be made for the 10 minutes interval between innings.

If an innings ends or there is a stoppage caused by weather or bad light within 30 minutes of the agreed time for the tea interval, the interval shall be taken immediately. The interval shall be of the agreed length and, if applicable, shall include the 10 minute interval between innings. If at the agreed time for the tea interval, nine wickets are down, play shall continue for a period not exceeding 30 minutes or until the innings is concluded. At any time during the match, the Captains may agree to forego a tea interval. If both Captains agree before the start of a match that intervals for drinks may be taken, the option to take such intervals shall be available to either side. These intervals shall be restricted to one per session, shall be kept as short as possible, shall not be taken in the last hour of the match and in any case shall not exceed 5 minute The agreed times for these intervals shall be strictly adhered to except that if a wicket falls within 5 minutes of the agree time then drinks shall be taken out immediately.

If an innings ends or there is a stoppage caused by weather or bad light within 30 minutes of the agreed time for a drinks interval, there will be no interval for drinks in that session. At any time during the match the Captains may agree to forego any such drinks interval.

Cessation of play

The Umpire at Bowler's end shall call "time) on the cessation of play before any interval or interruption of play, at the end of each day's play, and at the conclusion of the match. After the call of "time", the Umpires shall remove the bails from both wickets. The last over before an interval or the close of play shall be started provided the Umpire, after walking at his normal pace, has arrived at his position behind the stumps at the Bowler's end before time has been reached. An over before an interval or the close of play shall be completed unless a Batsman is out or retires during that over within 2 minutes of the interval or the close of play or unless the players have occasion to leave the field. An over in progress at the close of play on the final day of a match shall be completed at the request of either Captain even if a wicket falls after time has been reached.

If during the last over the players have occasion to leave the field the Umpires shall call "time" and there shall be no resumption of play and the match shall be at an end. The Umpires shall indicate when one hour of playing time of the match remains according to the agreed hours of play. The next over after that moment shall be the first of a minimum of 20 6 ball overs, (15-8-ball overs), provided a result is not reached earlier or there is no interruption of play.

If, at the commencement of the last hour of the match, an interval between innings or an interruption of play shall be reduced in proportion to the duration, with the last hour of the match, of any such interval or interruption.

The minimum number of overs to be bowled after a resumption of play shall be calculated as follows:

(a) In the case of an interval or interruption of play being in progress at the commencement of the last hour of the match, or in the case of a first interval or interruption a deduction shall be made from the minimum of 20 6-ball overs (or 15 8-ball overs).

(b) If there is a later interval or interruption a further deduction shall be made from the minimum number of overs which should have been bowled following the last resumption of play.

(c) These deductions shall be based on the following factors:

(i) The number of overs already bowled in the last hour of the match or, in the case of a later interval or interruption in the last session of play.

(ii) The number of overs lost as a result of the interval or interruption allowing one 6-ball over for every full 4 minutes (or one 6-ball over for every full four minutes) if interval or interruption.

(iii) Any over left uncompleted at the end of an innings to be excluded from these calculation.

(iv) Any over left uncompleted at the start of an interruption of play to be completed when play is resumed and to count as one over bowled.

(v) An interval to start with the end of an innings and to end 10 minutes later an interruption to start on the call of 'time' and to end on the call 'play'.

(d) In the event of an innings being completed and an a new innings commencing during the last hour of the match, the number of overs to be bowled to the new innings shall be calculated on the basis of one-6ball over for every four minutes or part there of remaining for play (or one 8-ball over for every four minutes or part there of remaining for play); or alternatively on the basis that sufficient overs be bowled to enable the full minimum quota of overs to be completed under circumstances governed by (a), (b), and (c) above. In all such cases the alternative which allows the greater number of overs shall be employed.

Scoring

The score shall be reckoned by runs. A run is scored:-

(a) So often as the Batsmen, after a hit or at any time while the ball is in play, shall have crossed and made good their ground from end to end.

(b) When a boundary is scored.

(c) When penalty runs are awarded.

Short Runs

(a) If either Batsman runs a short run, the Umpire shall call and signal "one short" as soon as the ball becomes dead and that run shall not be scored. A run is short if a Batsman fails to make good his ground on turning for a further run.

(b) Although a short run shortens the succeeding one, the latter, if completed shall count.

(c) If either or both Batsmen deliberately run short the Umpire shall, as soon as he sees that the fielding side have no chance of dismissing either Batsman, call and signal "dead ball" and disallow any runs attempted or previously scored. The Batsmen shall return to their original ends.

(d) If both Batsmen run short in one and the same run, only one run shall be deducted.

(e) Only if three or more runs are attempted can more than one be short and then, subject to (c) and (d) above, all runs so called shall be disallowed. If there has been more than one short run the Umpires shall instruct the Scorers as to the number of runs disallowed.

If the striker is caught, no run shall be scored. If a Batsman is run Out, only that run which was being attempted shall not be scored. If, however, an injured striker himself is run out not runs shall be scored.

If a Batsman is out Obstructing the Field, any runs completed before the obstruction occurs shall be scored unless such obstruction prevents a catch being made in which case no runs shall be scored.

Boundaries

Before the toss for innings, the Umpires shall agree with both Captains on the boundary of the playing area. The boundary shall, if possible, be, marked by a white line, a rope laid on the ground, or a fence. If flags or posts only are used to mark a boundary, the imaginary line joining such points shall be regarded as the boundary. An obstacle, or person, within the playing area shall not be regarded as a boundary unless so decided by the Umpires before the toss for innings. Sight-screens within, or partially within, the playing area shall be regarded as the boundary and when the ball strikes or passes within or under or directly over any part of the screen, a boundary shall be scored.

Before the toss for innings, the Umpires shall agree with both Captains the runs to be allowed for boundaries, and in deciding the allowance for them, the Umpires and Captains shall be guided by the prevailing custom of the ground. The allowance for a boundary shall normally be 4 runs, and 6 runs for all hits pitching over and clear of the boundary line or fence, even though the ball has been previously touched by a Fieldsman 6 runs shall also be scored if a

Fieldsman, after catching a ball, carries it over the boundary.

A boundary shall be scored and signalled by the Umpire at the Bowler's end whenever, in his opinion:

(a) A ball in play touches or crosses the boundary, however marked.

(b) A fieldsman with ball in hand touches or grounds any part of his person on or over a boundary line.

(c) A Fieldsman with ball in hand grounds any part of his person over a boundary fence or board. This allows the Fieldsman to touch or lean on or over a boundary fence or board in preventing a boundary.

The runs completed at the instant the ball reaches the boundary shall count if they exceed the boundary allowance. If the boundary results from an overthrow or from the wilful act of a Fieldsman, any run already completed and the allowance shall be added to the score. The run in progress shall count provided that the Batsmen have crossed at the instant of the throw or act.

Lost ball

If a ball in play cannot be found or recovered any fieldsman may call "lost ball" when 6 runs shall be added to the score; but if more than 6 have been run before "lost ball" is called, as many runs as have been completed shall be scored. The run in progress shall count provided that the Batsmen have crossed at the instant of the call of "lost ball".

The runs shall be added to the score of the striker if the ball has been struck, but otherwise to the score of byes, leg-byes, no- balls or wides as the case may be.

The result

The side which has scored a total of runs in excess of that scored by the opposing side in its two completed innings shall be the winners.

(a) One innings matches, unless played out as in 1. above, shall be decided on the first innings.

(b) If the Captains agree to continue play after the completion of one innings of each side in accordance with law and a result is not achieved on the second innings, the first innings result shall stand.

Umpires awarding a match

(a) A Match shall be lost by a side which, during the match.

(i) refuses to play, or

(ii) concedes defeat,

and the Umpires shall award the march to the other side.

(b) Should both Batsmen at the wickets or the fielding side leave the field at any time without the agreement of the Umpires, this shall constitute a refusal to play and, on appeal, the Umpires shall award the match to the other side in accordance with (a) above.

The result of a match shall be a tie when the scores are equal at the conclusion of play, but only if the side batting last has completed its innings. If the scores of the completed first innings of a one-day match are equal, it shall be a tie but only if the match has not been played out to a further conclusion. A match not determined in any of the ways as in 1,2,3 and 4 above shall count as a draw. Any decision as to the correctness of the scores shall be the responsibility of the Umpires. If, after the Umpires and players have left the field, in the belief that the match has been concluded, the Umpires decide that a mistake in scoring has occurred, which affects the result, and provided time has not been reached, they shall order play to resume and to continue until the agreed finishing time unless a result is reached earlier.

If the Umpires decide that a mistake has occurred and time has been reached, the Umpires shall immediately inform both Captains of the necessary correction to the scores and, if applicable, to the result. In accepting the scores as notified by the scores and agreed by the Umpires, the Captains of both sides thereby accept the result.

The Over

The ball shall be bowled from each wicket alternately in overs of either 6 or 8 balls according to agreement before the match. When the agreed number of balls has been bowled, and as the ball becomes dead or when it becomes clear to the Umpire at the Bowler's end that both the fielding side and the Batsmen at the wicket have ceased to regard the ball as in play, the Umpire shall call "Over" before leaving the wicket. Neither a no ball nor a wide ball shall be reckoned as one of the over. If an Umpire miscounts the number of balls, the over as counted by the Umpire shall stand.

A Bowler shall be allowed to change ends as often as desired provided only that he does not bowl two overs consecutively in an innings. A bowler shall finish an over in progress unless he be incapacitated or be suspended. If an over is left incomplete for any reason at the start of an interval or interruption of play, it shall be finished on the resumption of play.

If for any reason, a Bowler incapacitated while running up to bowl the first ball of an over, the Umpire shall call and signal "dead ball" and another Bowler shall be allowed to bawl or complete the over from the same end, provided only that he shall not bawl two overs, or part thereof, consecutively in one innings.

The Batsman at the Bowler's end shall normally stand on the opposite side of the wicket to that from which the ball is being delivered, unless a request to do otherwise is granted by the Umpire.

Dead ball

The Ball becomes dead, when:

(a) It is finally settled in the hands of the Wicket Keeper or the Bowler.

(b) It reaches or pitches over the boundary.

(c) A Batsman is out.

(d) Whether played or not, it lodges in the clothing or equipment of a Batsman of the clothing of an Umpire.

(e) A ball lodges in a protective helmet worn by a member of the fielding side.

(f) A penalty is awarded

(g) The Umpire calls "over" or " time".

Either Umpire Shall Call and Signal "Dead Ball", when: (a) He intervenes in a case of unfair play.

(b) A serious injury to a player or Umpire occurs.

(c) He is satisfied that, for an adequate reason, the Striker is not ready to receive the ball and makes no attempt to play it.

(d) The Bowler drops the ball accidentally before delivery, or the ball does not leave his hand for any reason.

(e) One or both bails fall from the striker's wicket before he receives delivery.

(f) He leaves his normal position for consultation.

The Ball Ceases to be Dead, when:

(a) The Bowler starts his run up or bowling action.

The Ball is Not Dead, when:

(a) It strikes an Umpire (unless it lodges in his dress).

(b) The wicket is broken or struck down (unless a Batsman is out thereby).

(c) An unsuccessful appeal is made.

(d) The wicket is broken accidentally either by the Bowler during his delivery or by a Batsman in running.

(e) The Umpire has called "no ball", or 'wide'.

No ball

The Umpire shall indicate to the striker whether the Bowler intends to bowl over or round the wicket, overarm, or right or left- handed. Failure on the part of the Bowler to indicate in advance a change in his mod of delivery is unfair and the Umpire shall call and signal "on ball". The Umpire at tne bowler's end shall call and signal 'No Ball Which the Umpire considers to have been delivered:-

(i) bounces "more" than twice or

(ii) rolls along the ground or

(iii)comes to rest before it reaches the striker' or if not otherwise played by the striker before it reaches the popping crease.

If the ball comes to rest in such circumstance, the striker has a right without interference from the fielding side, to make one attempt to hit the ball. If the fielding side interferes, the Umpire shall replace the ball where it came to rest and shall order the fieldsmen to resume the places they occupied in the field before the ball was delivered.

The Umpire shall call and signal 'Dead Ball' as soon as it is clear that the striker does not intend to hit the ball or after the striker has made an unsuccessful attempt to hit the ball.

It is accepted that this wording is very lengthy, but it is felt that it covets adequately the occasional problem of a bowler delivering a ball along the ground in order to prevent the possibility of a 'six' being hit, without having to disallow any bowler from delivering the ball underarm. If this regulation is accepted, the question of whether or not a batsman can be caught after hitting a ball which has come to rest does not apply, since it would be a 'No Ball'.

For a delivery to the fair the ball must be bowled no thrown. The Umpire at the bowler's wicket shall call and signal "no ball" if he is not satisfied that in the delivery stride:

(a) The Bowler's back foot has landed within and not touching the return crease or its forward extension

Or

(b) Some part of the front foot whether grounded or raised was behind the popping crease.

If the Bowler, before delivering the ball, throws it at the striker's wicket in an attempt to run him out, the Umpire shall call and signal "no ball". If the Bowler, before delivering the ball, attempts the ball, attempts to run out the non- striker, any runs which result shall be allowed and shall be scored as no balls. Such an attempt shall not count as a ball in the over. The Umpire shall not call :no ball". An Umpire shall revoke the call "no ball" if the ball does not leave the Bowler's hand for any reason. A penalty of one run for a no ball shall be scored if no runs are made otherwise.

The striker may hit a no ball and whatever runs result shall be added to his score. Runs made otherwise from a no ball shall be scored no balls.

Should a Batsman be given out off a no ball the penalty for bowling it shall stand unless runs are otherwise scored.

Wide Ball

If the Bowler bowls the ball so high over or so wide of the wicket that, in the opinion of the Umpire it passes out of reach of the striker, standing in a normal guard position, the Umpire shall call and signal "wide ball" as soon as it has passed the line of the striker's wicket.

The Umpire shall not adjudge a ball as being a wide if:

(a) The Striker, by moving from his guard position,

causes the ball to pass out of his reach.

(b) The Striker moves and thus brings the ball within his reach.

A penalty of one run for a wide shall be scored if no runs are made otherwise. The Umpire shall revoke the call if the Striker hits a ball which has been called "wide". The ball does not become dead on the call of "wide ball". All runs which are run or result from a wide ball which is not a no ball shall be scored wide balls, or if no runs are made one shall be scored. Should a Batsman be given out off a wide, the penalty for bowling it shall stand unless runs are otherwise made.

Bay and Leg-bye

If the ball, not having been called "wide" or "no ball" passes the striker without touching his bat or person, and any runs are obtained, the Umpire shall signal "bye" and the run or runs shall be credited as such to the batting side. If the ball, not having been called "wide" or "no ball" is unintentionally deflected by the striker's dress or person, except a hand holding the bat, and any runs are obtained the Umpire shall signal "leg-bye" and the run or runs so scored shall be credited as such to the batting side. Such leg-byes shall only be scored if, in the opinion of the Umpire, the striker has:

(a) attempted to play the ball with his bat, or

(b) tried to avoid being hit by the ball.

In the case of a deflection by the striker's person, other than in 2 (a) and (b) above, the Umpire shall call and signal "dead ball" as soon as one run has been completed or when it is clear that a run is not being attempted or the ball has reached the boundary. On the call and signal of "dead ball" the Batsmen small return to their original ends and no runs shall be allowed.

Appeals

The Umpires shall not give a Batsman out unless appealed to by other side which shall be done prior to the Bowler beginning his run up or bowling action to deliver the next ball. Under *the ball is dead* on "over" being called; this does not, however, invalidate an appeal made prior to the following over provided 'time' has not been called. An Appeal "How's That?": Shall cover all ways of being out. When either Umpire has given a Batsman not out, the other Umpire shall within his jurisdiction, answer the appeal or a further appeal, provided it is made in them in accordance with.

An Umpire may consult with the other Umpire on point of fact which the latter may have been in a better position to see and shall then give his decision shall be in favour of the Batsman.

The Umpires shall intervene if satisfied that a Batsman, not having been given out, has left his wicket under a misapprehension that he has been dismissed.

The Umpire's decision is final. He may alter his decision, provided that such alteration is made promptly. In exceptional circumstances the Captain of the fielding side may seek permission of the Umpire to withdraw an appeal provision the outgoing Batsman has not left the playing area. If this is allowed, the Umpire shall cancel his decision.

The wicket is down

The wicket is down if:

(a) Either the ball or the Striker's bat or person completely removes either bail from the top of the stumps. A disturbance of a bail, whether temporary or not shall not constitute a complete removal, but the wicket is down if a bail in falling lodges between two of the stumps.

(b) Any player completely removes with his hand or arm a bail from the top of the stumps, provided that the ball is held in that hand or in the hand of the arm so used.

(c) When both bail are off, a stump is struck out of the ground by the ball, or a player strikes or pulls a stump out of the ground, provided that the ball is held in the hand(s) or in the hand of the arm so used.

If bail is off, it shall be sufficient for the purpose of putting the wicket down to remove the remaining bail, or to strike or pull any of the three stumps out of the ground in any of the ways stated above.

If all the stumps are out of the ground, the fielding, side shall be allowed to put back one or more stumps in order to have an opportunity of putting the wicket down. If owing to the strength of the wind, it has been agreed to dispense with the bails in accordance with.

Batsman out of his ground

A Batsman shall be considered to be out of his ground unless some part of his bat in his hand or of his person is ground behind the line of the popping crease.

Bowled

The striker shall be out bowled if:

(a) His wicket is bowled down, even if the ball first touches his bat or person.

(b) He breaks his wicket by hitting or kicking the ball on to it before the completion of a stroke, or as a result of attempting to guard his wicket.

Timed out

An incoming Batsman shall be out Time Out if he willfully takes more than two minutes to come in—the two minutes being timed of play. If this is not complied with and if the Umpire is satisfied that the delay was wilful and if an appeal is made, the new Batsman shall be given out by the Umpire at the Bowler's end. The time taken by the Umpires to investigate the cause the delay shall be added to the normal close of play.

Caught

The striker shall be out Caught if the ball touches his bat or if touches below the wrist his hand or glove, holding the bat, and is subsequently held by a Fieldsman before it touches the ground.

A catch shall be considered to have been fairly made if:

(a) The Fieldsman is within the field of play throughout the act of making the catch.

(i) The act of making the catch shall start from the time when the Fieldsman first handles the ball and shall end when he both retains complete control over the further disposal of the ball and remains within the field of play.

(ii) In order to be within the field of play, the Fieldsman may not touch or ground any part of his person on or over a boundary line. When the boundary is marked by a fence or board the Fieldsman may not ground any part of his person over the boundary fence or board, but may touch or lean over the boundary fence or board in completing the catch.

(b) The ball is hugged to the body of the catcher or accidentally lodges in his dress or, in the case of the Wicket-Keeper, in his pads,. However a striker may not be caught if a ball lodges in a protective helmet worn by a Fieldsman. in which case the Umpire shall call and signal "dead ball".

(c) The ball does not touch the ground even though a hand holding it does so in effecting the catch.

(d) A Fieldsman catches the ball after it has been lawfully played a second time by the striker, but only if the ball has not touched the ground since being first struck.

(e) A Fieldsman catches the ball after it has touched an Umpire, another Fieldsman or the other Batsman. However a striker may not be caught if a ball has touched a protective helmet worn by a Fieldsman.

(f) The ball is caught off an obstruction within the boundary provided it has not previously been agreed to regard the obstruction as a boundary.

If a striker is caught, no runs shall be scored.

Handled the ball

Either Batsman on appeal shall be out Handled the Ball if he wilfully touches the ball while in play with the hand not holding the bat unless he does so with the consent of the opposite side.

Hit the ball twice

The striker, on appeal, shall be out Hit the Ball Twice if, after the ball is struck or is stopped by any part of his person, he willfully strikes it again with his bat or person except for the sole purpose of guarding this wicket this he may do with his bat or any part of his person other than this hands. For the purpose of this, a hand holding the bat shall be regarded as part of the bat. The striker, on appeal, shall be out under this law, if, without the consent of the opposite side, he uses his bat or person to return the ball to any of the fielding side.

Hit wicket

The striker shall be out Hit Wicket if, while the ball is in play:-

(a) His wicket is broken with any part of his person, dress, or equipment as a result of action taken by him in preparing to receive or in receiving a delivery, or in setting off for his first run, immediately after playing, or playing at, the ball.

(b) He hits down his wicket whilst lawfully making a second stroke for the purpose of guarding his wicket within the provision of Law.

Leg before wicket

The striker shall be out L.B.W. in the circumstances set out below:

(a) Striker Attempting to play the Ball

The striker shall be out L.B.W. if he first intercepts

with any part of his person, dress or equipment a fair ball which would have hit the wicket and which has not previously touched his bat or a hand holding the bat, provided that:

(i) The ball pitched, in a straight line between wicket and wicket or one the off side of the Stricker's wicket, or in the case of a ball intercepted full pitch would have pitched in a straight line between wicket and wicket and

(ii) The point of impact is in a straight line between wicket and wicket, even if above the level of the bails.

(b) Striker making no attempt to play the ball

The striker shall be out LBW even if the ball is intercepted outside the line of the off-stump, if, in the opinion of the Umpire, he has made no genuine attempt to play the ball with his bat, but has intercepted the ball with some part of his person and if the circumstances set out in (a) above apply.

Obstructing the field

Either Batsman, on appeal, shall be out obstructing the Field if he wilfully obstructs the opposite side by word or action.

The striker, on appeal, shall be out should wilful obstruction by either Batsman prevent a catch being made. This shall apply even though the striker causes the obstruction in lawfully guarding his wicket under the provisions of Law.

Run out

Either Batsman shall be out Run Out if in running or at

any time while the ball is in play—except in the circumstances described—he is out of his ground and his wicket is put down by the opposite side. If, however, a Batsman in running makes good his ground he shall not be out Run Out, if he subsequently leaves his ground, in order to avoid injury, and the wicket is put down. If a no ball has been called, the Striker shall not be given Run Out unless he attempts to run. If the Batsmen have crossed in running, he who runs for the wicket which is put sown shall be out; if a Batsman remains in his ground or returns to his ground and the other Batsman joins him there, the latter shall be out if his wicket is put down. If a Batsman is run out, only that run which is being attempted shall not be scored.

Stumped

The striker shall be out stumped if, in receiving a ball, not being a no-ball, he is out of his ground otherwise than in attempting a run and the wicket is put down by the Wicket Keeper may take the ball in front of the wicket in an attempt to stump the striker only if the ball has touched the bat or person of the striker.

The wicket-keeper

The wicket-Keeper shall remain wholly behind the wicket until a ball delivered by the Bowler touches the bat or person of the striker, or passes the wicket, or until the striker attempts a run.

In the event of the Wicket-Keeper contravening this law, the Umpire at the striker's end shall call and signal "no ball" at the instant of delivery or as possible thereafter. If the Wicket-Keeper interferes with the striker's right to play the ball and to guard his wicket, the striker shall not be out. Interference with the Wicket-Keeper by the Striker: If in the legitimate defence of his wicket, the striker interferes with the Wicket-Keeper.

The fieldsman

The Fieldsman may stop the ball with any part of his person, but if he wilfully stops it otherwise, 5 runs shall be added to the run or runs already scored; if no run has been scored 5 penalty runs shall be awarded. The run in progress shall count provided that the Batsman have crossed at the instant of the act. If the ball has been struck, the penalty shall be added to the score of the striker, but otherwise to the score of byes, leg-byes, no balls or wides as the case may be. The number of on-side Fieldsmen behind the popping crease at the instant of the Bowler's devlivery shall not exceed two. In the event of infringement by the fielding side the Umpire at the Striker's end shall call and singal "no ball" at the instant of delivery or as soon as possible thereafter. Whilst the ball is in play and until the ball has made contact with the bat or the striker's person or has passed his bat, no Fieldsman, other than the Bowler, may stand on or have any part of his person extended over the pitch (measuring 22 yards/20.12 m. x10 ft./3.05 m.). In the event of a Fieldsman contravening this Law, the Umpire at the bowler's end shall call and signal" no ball" at the instant of delivery or as soon as possible thereafter.

Protective Helmets, when not in use by members of the fielding side, shall only be placed, if above the surface, on the ground behind the Wicket-Keeper.

Unfair play

The Captains are responsible at all times for ensuring that play is conducted within the spirit of the game as well as within the Laws. The Umpire are the sole judges of fair and unfair play. The Umpires shall intervene without appeal by calling and signalling "dead ball" in the case of unfair play, but should not otherwise interfere with the progress of the game except as required to do so by the Laws. A player shall not lift the seam of the ball for any reason. Should this be done, the Umpires shall change the ball for one of similar condition to that in use prior to the contravention.

Any member of the fielding side polish the ball provided that such polishing wastes no time and that no artificial substance is used. No-One shall rub the ball one the ground or use any artificial substance or take any other action to alter the condition of the ball. In the event of a contravention of this Law, the Umpires, after consultation, shall change the ball for one of similar condition to that in use prior to the contravention.

This Law does not prevent a member of the fielding side from drying a wet ball, or removing mud from the ball. An Umpire is justified in intervening under this Law and shall call and signal "dead ball" if, in his opinion, any player of the fielding side incommodes the striker by any noise or action while he is receiving a ball.

It shall be considered unfair if any Fieldsman wilfully obstructs a Batsman in running. In these circumstance the Umpire shall call and signal "dead ball" and allow any completed runs and the run in progress or alternatively any boundary scored. The bowling of fast short pitched balls is unfair if, in the opinion of the Umpire at the Bowler's end, it constitutes an attempt to intimidate the striker. Umpire shall consider intimidation to be the deliberate bowling of fast short pitched balls which by their length, height and direction are intended or likely to inflict physical injury on the Striker. The relative skill of the striker shall also be taken into consideration.

In the event of such unfair bowling, the Umpire at the Bowler's end shall adopt the following procedure.

(a) In the first instance the Umpire shall call and signal "no ball", caution the Bowler and inform the other Umpire, the Captain of the fielding side and the Batsman of what has occurred.

(b) If this caution is ineffective, he shall repeat the above procedure and indicate to the Bowler that this is a final warning.

(c) Both the above caution and final warning shall continue to apply even though the Bowler may later change ends.

(d) Should the above warnings prove ineffective the Umpire at the Bowler's end shall:

(i) At the first repetition call and signal "no ball" and when the ball is dead direct the Captains to take the Bowler off forthwith and to complete the over with another Bowler, provided that the Bowler does not bowl two overs or part thereof consecutively.

(ii) Not allow the Bowler, thus taken off, to bowl again in the same innings.

(iii) Report the occurrence to the Captain of the batting side as soon as the player leave the field for an interval.

(iv) Report the occurrence to the Executive of the fielding side and to any governing body responsible for the match who shall take any further action which is considered to be appropriate against the Bowler concerned.

The bowling of fast high full pitches is unfair. In the event of such unfair bowling the Umpire at the bowler's end shall adopt the procedures of caution, final warning, action against the Bowler and reporting as set out in 8. above.

Any form of time wasting is unfair.

(a) In the event of the Captain of the fielding side wasting time or allowing any member of his side to waste time, the Umpire at the Bowler's end shall adopt the following procedure:

(i) In the first instance he shall caution the Captain of the fielding side and inform the other Umpire of what has occurred.

(ii) If this caution is ineffective he shall repeat the above procedure and indicate to the Captain that this is a final warning.

(iii) The Umpire shall report the occurrence to the Captain of the batting side as soon as the players leave the field for an interval.

(iv) Should the above procedure prove ineffective the Umpire shall report the occurrence to the Executive of the fielding side and to any governing body responsible for that match who shall take appropriate action against the Captain and the players concerned.

(b) In the event of a Bowler taking unnecessarily long to bowl an over the Umpire at the Bowler's end shall adopt the procedures, other than the calling of "no-ball", of caution, final warning, action against the Bowler and reporting.

(c) In the event of a Batsman wasting time other than in the manner described, the Umpire at the Bowler's and shall adopt the following procedure:

(i) In the first instance he shall caution the Batsman and inform the other Umpire at once, and the Captain of the batting side, as soon as the players leave the field for an interval, of what has occurred.

(ii) If this proves ineffective, he shall repeat the caution, indicate to the Batsman that this is a final warning and inform the other Umpire.

(iii)The Umpire shall report the occurrence to both Captains as soon as the players leave the field for an interval.

(iv)Should the above procedure prove ineffective, the Umpire shall report the occurrence to the Executive of the batting side and to any governing body responsible for that match who shall take appropriate action against the player concerned.

The Umpires shall intervene and prevent players from causing damage to the pitch which may assist the Bowlers of either side.

(a) In the event of any member of the fielding side damaging the pitch the Umpire shall follow the Procedure of caution, final warning and reporting as set out in 10 (a) above.

(b) In the event of a Bowler contravening this Law by running sown the pitch after delivering the ball, the Umpire at the Bowler's end shall first caution the Bowler. If this caution is ineffective the Umpire shall adopt the procedures, other than the calling of "no-ball", of final warning, action against the Bowler and repotting.

(c) In the event of a Batsman damaging the pitch the Umpire at the Bowler's end shall follow the procedures of caution, final warning and reporting as set out in 10 (c) above.

Any attempt by the Batsman to steal a run during the Bowler's run-up is unfair. Unless the Bowler attempts to run out either Batsman—the Umpire shall call and signal "dead ball" as soon as the Batsmen cross in any such attempt to run. The Batsman shall then return to their original wickets. In the event of a player failing to comply with the instructions of an Umpire, criticising his decisions by word or action, or showing dissent, or generally behaving in a manner which might bring the game into disrepute, the Umpire concerned shall, in the first place report the matter to the other Umpire and to the player's Captain requesting the latter to take action. If this proves ineffective, the Umpire shall report the incident as soon as possible to the Executive of the player's team and to any Governing Body responsible for the match, who shall take any further action which is considered appropriate against the player or players concerned.

INDEX